I0017387

Contents

Introduction

The ever-changing nature of modern cyber-attacks includes emerging threats like internet of things devices and deep fakes. Organizations must regularly assess the threat landscape, adapt cybersecurity measures, and consider investing in new technologies. I'll provide insights into common and emerging threats, along with strategies for protection. The threat landscape varies among organizations, but understanding it is crucial, as every organization will likely face these threats sooner or later.

When establishing a cybersecurity program, it's essential to address diverse requirements from customers, regulators, and internal stakeholders. We will learn a practical managerial approach emphasizing data-driven decision-making and proactive measures. The focus is on orchestrating people, procedures, policy, and technology to safeguard data and corporate assets. Join to adopt an effective strategy against cyber threats.

Understanding and communicating the status of cybersecurity can be challenging, especially when seeking funding. Utilizing security metrics is the key to addressing this issue. These metrics offer insights into the current state of a cybersecurity program, crucial for driving improvement and establishing a standard for effective communication. Security metrics serve as a valuable tool for sharing information with auditors, customers, and partners. Learning how to use security metrics allows you to showcase your team's value, build trust, and secure the budget you need. The primary purpose of security metrics is to enhance the maturity and effectiveness of cybersecurity activities. Leveraging measurements and data enables you to address broken processes, prioritize critical controls, and ensure the success of fundamental security principles.

Organizations increasingly recognize the importance of a Chief Information Security Officer (CISO) as an executive leader capable of making critical security decisions and educating the management team and other leaders about relevant risks. We will share practical insights to assist participants in collaborating effectively with their executive leadership teams.

Senior decision-makers globally face the challenge of managing extensive cyber risks with constrained budgets and staffing. Effectively running a cybersecurity program involves numerous tasks, but attracting and retaining qualified personnel is a major obstacle. Amidst this, there is pressure to control headcount growth. To navigate this situation, setting priorities and making tough choices is essential. One pivotal decision is whether and how to outsource. In our discussion, we'll offer insights and practical steps to help you assess the suitability of outsourcing cybersecurity tasks and guide you on how to proceed. Whether you have experience with outsourcing or are considering it for the first time, our insights aim to ensure your success.

You might be facing challenges in attracting and retaining cybersecurity talent in a competitive job market. We'll explore the strategy of focusing on entry-level talent to address the skills gap. Discover how building a pipeline of newcomers can strengthen your talent pool, enhance your security program, and offer a better return on investment. I'll guide you through the benefits of providing opportunities to individuals early in their careers, as it has played a crucial role in my own professional journey.

Security awareness involves consciously recognizing, understanding, or having knowledge about security, encompassing both logical and physical aspects in cybersecurity. The program aims to impart effective knowledge to employees about security risks and threats, enabling them to recognize, combat, and prevent these risks. It goes beyond education and training, requiring cultural change with top-down and bottom-up buy-in, becoming a credible, relatable, and integral part of the company. A mature security awareness program is crucial for protecting employees and company assets. It facilitates change through awareness, communications, training, and education, providing effective tools to combat cyber threats. Developing and leading such a program requires passion for security, understanding of learning styles, and excellent communication skills, with soft skills being imperative. The process may involve challenges, but the rewarding outcome of creating positive security change in the organization makes it worthwhile.

A cyber-attack, like ransomware, poses a significant threat, potentially crippling your network and tarnishing your reputation. Regardless of your company's size, the interconnected nature of today's economy necessitates preparation for such incidents before they occur. I'll guide you through a practical strategy for communicating during a cyber-attack crisis. Topics covered include understanding the impact of cyber-attacks, outlining response steps for ransomware and other breaches, and providing insights on evaluation and training both before and after an attack.

Chapter 1 The Cybersecurity Threat Landscape

Explore the threat of malware and ransomware

Malware, a persistent cybersecurity threat since the late 1980s, encompasses various harmful software types aiming to gain unauthorized access and cause damage, extract information, or generate profits for attackers. One prevalent form, ransomware, encrypts data and demands payment for recovery. Both malware and ransomware exploit system vulnerabilities or trick users through social engineering, posing significant risks to individuals and organizations. The infection methods, including phishing attacks, persist despite available patches, contributing to the ongoing cybersecurity threat landscape. Ransomware, in particular, attracts attention due to its lucrative nature, with reported victims in the U.S. facing over $29.1 million in losses in 2020 alone. As long as vulnerabilities persist and users succumb to social engineering tactics, malware and ransomware will remain formidable elements in the cybersecurity landscape.

Protect against malware and ransomware

To mitigate the severe impact of malware or ransomware attacks on individuals and organizations, implementing simple protective measures is crucial. Here are five key steps to enhance defense:

1. Frequent Backups: Regularly back up your data to minimize the impact of compromised systems. This is especially critical for recovering from targeted ransomware attacks on your data. Ensure you test backups to confirm their integrity.

2. Apply Security Updates and Patches: Reduce vulnerability by regularly updating and patching your systems. This proactive measure significantly lowers the risk of malware and ransomware attacks.

3. Upgrade Operating Systems: Stay current with the latest operating system versions to enhance security, as newer versions are often more resilient to threats. Avoid exposing your systems to vulnerabilities that lack patches.

4. Install Firewalls: Use firewalls, both hardware and software, to prevent unauthorized access. This is essential for safeguarding systems directly connected to the internet and blocking malicious communication attempts.

5. Install Anti-Malware Software: Protect against accidental malware introductions through social engineering by installing anti-malware software on all systems. Ensure regular updates of malware signatures to maintain effectiveness.

By adhering to these security controls, you can significantly reduce the risk of malware and ransomware exposure.

Explore the threat of phishing and smishing

Phishing and smishing are social engineering tactics aimed at deceiving users into divulging sensitive information like usernames, passwords, and credit card details. Phishing, an enduring threat since the 1990s, involves sending fraudulent emails, often appearing urgent, with manipulated links or malicious attachments. The goal is to make users enter their credentials on forged websites. Spear phishing tailors' attacks to specific users, leveraging familiarity. Smishing, similar to phishing, utilizes SMS texts impersonating trusted entities, such as banks or colleagues, to trick users into revealing information or performing tasks that benefit the attackers. Given their cost-effectiveness and simplicity, these attacks are anticipated to persist as prominent threats in the cybersecurity landscape.

Protect against phishing and smishing

While phishing remains a prevalent cybersecurity threat, there are effective measures to reduce vulnerability. Five key steps include:

1. Email Filtering Controls: Enhance protection by implementing controls that filter and block malicious emails. Users can mark suspicious emails as junk, and organizations can blacklist known malicious servers, domains, or IP addresses.

2. Block Access to Malicious Websites: Prevent access to fraudulent sites at both user and organizational levels. Configure browsers for warnings, install firewalls, or use proxy servers to block known malicious websites.

3. Use a Password Manager: Employ a password manager to generate and store unique, strong passwords for different sites, minimizing the risk of password reuse in case of compromise.

4. Multifactor Authentication: Strengthen authentication with multifactor methods, requiring additional verification such as a device or biometric factor, beyond just passwords.

5. Security Training: Educate users on recognizing phishing threats, emphasizing caution with urgent emails and teaching techniques like hovering over links for legitimacy checks. Conduct phishing simulations to assess user awareness.

For smishing protection, security training is paramount. Instruct users on identifying suspicious text messages, avoiding link clicks, and confirming requests through alternative methods. Utilize smartphone settings to block unwanted text messages and explore additional filtering options. Implementing these controls enhances protection against phishing and smishing threats.

Explore the threat of business email compromise

Business Email Compromise (BEC) is a cybercrime with significant financial consequences for organizations. BEC attacks involve hackers gaining access to email accounts, often through spear phishing, and impersonating high-ranking executives or other trusted entities. The aim is to deceive employees into making large payments or altering payment processes, directing funds to the attacker's account. BEC attackers employ a combination of phishing, social engineering, and financial fraud. They may use additional tactics like deepfake audio to enhance the authenticity of their requests. While methods such as spoofed emails or lookalike domains are used, the most common variations of BEC attacks include false invoice scams, payroll diversion, CEO fraud, gift card scams, and home buyer fraud. Despite not being the most common, BEC is the highest cybercrime, with reported losses in the US reaching nearly $2.4 billion in 2021 alone, a 30% increase from the previous year. These losses are likely underestimated, given that they only account for reported cases in the US. The global appeal of high rewards, simplicity, and low risks associated with BEC attacks indicates that they will continue to be a significant cybersecurity threat.

Protect against business email compromise

Protecting against Business Email Compromise (BEC) involves similar measures as phishing prevention, with additional safeguards. Implement email filtering controls on your server to thwart email attacks targeting credential theft. Configure email protocols like SPF, DKIM, and DMARC to reduce domain spoofing attempts by BEC attackers. Enable multifactor authentication (MFA) on email accounts to enhance security, emphasizing its continuous use once activated. Conduct user security awareness training to educate users on recognizing BEC attacks, urging skepticism towards urgent or unusual fund transfer requests. Teach users to verify financial transaction requests through out-of-band methods and to scrutinize look-alike domains in emails. Add warning banners to external emails to alert users of potential email spoofing attempts. In case of a BEC incident, contact the financial institution promptly, report the crime to the local FBI field office (or equivalent law enforcement agency if outside the US), and file a complaint with the FBI's Internet Crime Complaint Center at ic3.gov. Implement these measures to reduce the risk of falling victim to BEC attacks in the evolving cybersecurity threat landscape.

Explore the threat of botnets and DDoS attacks

Botnets, not to be confused with sci-fi robots taking over, are collections of infected computers or IoT devices controlled remotely by malicious actors. These compromised systems, known as zombies, amplify attackers' capabilities, enabling various cyber-attacks. Among them, Distributed Denial of Service (DDoS) attacks stand out, aiming to overwhelm online services, particularly websites, with traffic from numerous sources. Botnets are used for DDoS attacks, spam campaigns, malware spreading, brute force attacks, and crypto mining. DDoS attacks, lasting hours to weeks, are often leveraged for extortion, with attackers demanding ransom to prevent or halt the assault. Some botnet operators even offer DDoS attacks as a service, allowing non-technical criminals to conduct such attacks easily. The proliferation of poorly secured internet-connected devices fuels the growth of botnets and DDoS attacks, ensuring their persistent presence in the cybersecurity threat landscape.

Protect against botnets and DDoS threats

While botnets and Distributed Denial of Service (DDoS) attacks pose growing threats in the cybersecurity landscape, there are effective ways to reduce exposure. For DDoS protection:

1. Implement firewalls or Web Application Firewalls (WAFs) to detect and block unwanted traffic.

2. Use load balancers or Content Delivery Networks (CDNs) to distribute traffic, diluting the impact of DDoS attacks.

3. Consider DDoS defense systems or specialized service providers like CloudFlare.

4. Employ a robust network monitoring system to detect unusual traffic and provide early warnings.

5. Develop a DDoS response plan, defining a response team and procedures for quick action.

To prevent systems from joining botnets:

1. Use effective anti-malware software with the latest definitions.

2. Monitor system processes for unusual or resource-intensive activity.

3. Implement strong password practices, keep software updated, and patch vulnerabilities.

4. Employ anti-spam controls on email servers, use web filtering to block malicious sites, and conduct regular user security awareness training.

These fundamental security measures go a long way in protecting systems from botnet and DDoS threats, considering the increasing scale and sophistication of these attacks.

Explore the threat of deepfakes

Deep fakes, driven by AI-based software, replicate voices and faces convincingly, seen in Hollywood and increasingly used by criminals in cyber-attacks. Instances include cloned CEO voices committing payment fraud in deep fake voice attacks, often combined with Business Email Compromise (BEC) tactics. Attackers employ email spoofs, followed by persuasive phone calls using deep fake audio, creating compelling scenarios for financial deception. With easily accessible deep fake audio applications and the difficulty of detecting fakes, particularly when ample target audio is available, these attacks pose a growing threat in the evolving cybersecurity landscape.

Protect against deepfakes

Detecting deep fakes becomes increasingly challenging with advancing AI technology, but there are strategies to identify and guard against them. Users should undergo training on deep fake technology, recognizing signs such as unnatural speech cadence, low-quality audio/video, digital artifacts, unnatural movement, blinking, lighting shifts, skin tone changes, and poor lip syncing. Red flags for social engineering include urgency and unusual behavior, prompting caution. Verification measures include confirming financial requests through alternate methods, calling back using official numbers, and posing test questions. Finance Departments should implement robust authorization processes for transactions. As deep fakes evolve, adopting these precautions becomes crucial for protecting individuals and organizations.

Explore the risk of insider threats

Internal threats within the cybersecurity landscape, often overlooked, can be as or even more perilous than external ones. Insiders encompass current/former employees, vendors, contractors, and business partners with privileged information. The danger lies in trusted insiders misusing their access, making detection challenging as they exploit legitimate pathways without breaching external controls. Malicious insider attacks involve sabotage, fraud, theft of sensitive data, and espionage. A real-world example involved a rogue software engineer hacking a cloud services provider, resulting in a $150 million incident. Unintentional insider threats stem from human error, bad judgment, falling for phishing or malware, or inadvertently aiding attackers. A case involved an employee emailing a spreadsheet with hidden sensitive data, leading to a costly security breach. Reports from the Ponemon Institute reveal rising costs of insider threats in North American companies, emphasizing the ongoing significance of this threat in the cybersecurity landscape.

Protect against insider threats

Protecting against insider threats is crucial yet challenging. Follow these four steps to fortify your organization. First, identify critical assets, ensuring their proper protection, monitoring, and reviewing access regularly. Develop and enforce policies, including an acceptable use policy, guidelines for admin account use, a transparent employee performance review process, a grievance resolution process, and a swift offboarding procedure. Implement technical security controls like monitoring user activities using a Security Information and Event Management (SIEM) system, adhering to the least privileged principle for access, reviewing privileges regularly, and utilizing network segmentation. Lastly, conduct user security awareness training, educating users on acceptable asset use, informing them about monitoring, emphasizing consequences of unauthorized activities, and encouraging reporting of any suspicious behavior.

Explore the threat of unmanaged IoT devices

The Internet of Things (IoT) poses significant cybersecurity threats such as data leaks, distributed denial of service attacks, and botnet-driven attacks. IoT's growth is driven by factors like cloud computing, affordable device costs, widespread use of smartphones for control, and easy Wi-Fi access. IoT devices encompass various electronics, from smart home appliances to health trackers and vehicles, projected to exceed 50 billion by 2025. However, these devices often lack adequate security measures, making them susceptible to automated attacks exploiting vulnerabilities. The Mirai botnet, using default passwords, exemplifies the potential threat, leading to large-scale DDoS attacks. Efforts are underway, like the IoT Cybersecurity Improvement Act, to establish security standards for IoT devices. Yet, as 5G and next-gen internet capabilities advance, IoT remains a significant player in the cybersecurity threat landscape.

Protect against unmanaged IoT devices

The proliferation of Internet of Things (IoT) devices brings a corresponding increase in security threats if deployed without proper safeguards. Despite challenges posed by poorly designed IoT devices, there are practical measures to safeguard your organization. Begin with an IT asset inventory and network scans to identify all devices, especially IoT ones. Network segmentation isolates critical assets from IoT devices, and blocking unnecessary ports, particularly Telnet port 23, enhances security. For easier-to-secure IoT devices, change default passwords, implement strong security configurations, and promptly install software updates and patches provided by manufacturers. Following security best practices, such as those outlined in OWASP's IoT top 10 vulnerabilities, will further fortify your defenses against unmanaged IoT threats.

Explore the threat of shadow IT

Most cybersecurity threats originate externally, but Shadow IT presents an internal challenge that is often unintentional. This phenomenon involves unauthorized use of systems, software, personal devices, or cloud services by employees. It arises when users bypass official IT channels due to perceptions of slow or restrictive IT practices or inadequate support. Shadow IT can account for a substantial portion of organizational spending, estimated at 30 to 40% by Gartner. Risks associated with Shadow IT include data loss, unpatched vulnerabilities, and a lack of security compliance. Enterprises face real dangers when unaware of or downplaying Shadow IT. As users continue to seek alternative IT solutions, Shadow IT will likely persist as a cybersecurity threat.

Protect against shadow IT

To mitigate the challenges of Shadow IT, consider implementing key controls and technologies. Start with fundamental controls, including maintaining an up-to-date IT asset inventory to identify unauthorized systems. Clearly communicate correct IT deployment processes to users, and enforce strong security policies that prohibit unauthorized IT solutions. Implement security monitoring systems like SIEM to detect and notify the IT team of unauthorized system additions. Explore network access control (NAC) to restrict network access to authorized systems only. Additionally, leverage Cloud Access Security Brokers (CASB) to enforce security controls on SaaS applications and monitor network traffic for potential shadow IT applications. These measures collectively reduce the risk and impact of shadow IT in your organization.

The threat of supply chain attacks and third-party risks

Every organization has an attack surface, and one significant area of exposure is through supply chains and third-party engagements. Supply chain risk arises from dependencies on suppliers, including technology providers, and their interconnected networks of suppliers. If a supplier fails, it can adversely affect the organization. Additionally, third parties like vendors and contractors, having access to an organization's systems, pose a risk, as demonstrated by a major retailer's security breach costing around $202 million. Storing critical data with third parties, especially in cloud-based applications, increases the risk of data accessibility by malicious actors. Software supply chain risk arises when organizations use open-source software, as vulnerabilities or malicious code can compromise systems, exemplified by the LOG4J vulnerability affecting millions of servers. Managing these complex risks is crucial due to their potential serious consequences for organizations.

Protect against supply chain attacks and third-party risks

Organizations often rely on supply chains and engage third parties for their operations, creating a substantial attack surface that requires protection. To mitigate these risks, establish a formal Third-Party Risk Management Program (TPRM). Develop an inventory of third-party suppliers, identify critical ones, and assess their access to your data and systems. Assign risk ratings based on business criticality and access, using these to prioritize alternatives and implement security controls. Follow the least privilege principle, mandate multifactor authentication, monitor third-party activity with a SIEM, promptly revoke unnecessary access, and verify third parties' security controls.

Collaborate with legal teams to incorporate strong security requirements in contracts. For software supply chain risk, conduct code inventories, create Software Bill of Materials (SBOMs), and review results with developers, emphasizing open-source software. Implement a secure development standard limiting outdated open-source software. While TPRM demands effort, it is crucial for managing and reducing supply chain and third-party risks.

Stay up to date on cybersecurity

After learning about common cybersecurity threats, the next step is to identify the relevant threats for your organization and ensure the corresponding security controls are in place. Stay informed by subscribing to security newsletters, podcasts, and magazines. Attend security conferences for in-depth insights and networking with professionals. Additionally, consider hiring cybersecurity professionals for threat simulation and management, including penetration tests and DDoS simulations. Stay vigilant and utilize the gained knowledge to protect against current and future threats.

Chapter 2 Building and Managing a Cybersecurity Program

Cybersecurity overview

Cybersecurity, a term introduced in 1994, has gained prominence, although its spelling remains debated. While often considered synonymous with information security, its definition varies. The National Institute of Standards and Technology defines it as safeguarding cyberspace from cyber-attacks, where we interpret cyberspace as the internet. For our focus, cybersecurity involves actions to minimize internet-related risks to an acceptable level for employers or customers.

Cyber resilience overview

Cyber resilience, defined as the ability to rebound after a cyber incident, is crucial due to rising online attacks. The increasing frequency of data breaches, with an average cost of $15.4 million for large companies, underscores the growing threat. Cybercriminals, now more organized and well-funded, target people and processes as security technologies improve. Newer threats, like business email compromise, have led to a global loss of over $43 billion. The emergence of cyber warriors, backed by nations like the US, Russia, and China, poses a sophisticated challenge. They exploit zero-day exploits, previously unknown software flaws, even infiltrating critical infrastructure. As major breaches become inevitable, focusing on cyber resilience is essential for organizations connected to the internet.

Risk management overview

Risk management involves dealing with uncertainties about the future and mitigating potential harm or loss. In the context of information and computer security, it addresses risks like cyber-attacks and data mishandling. Key questions include identifying vulnerabilities, determining risk levels, prioritizing risks, and implementing risk treatment options. These options, known as ACAT (Avoid, Control, Accept, Transfer), offer ways to manage risks effectively. While formal standards like ISO 31000 or NIST SP 800-30 can guide risk management, it's crucial to avoid becoming overly focused, paralyzed by perfectionism, or ineffective in communication. Accepting some level of risk is inherent, and simplicity and repeatability are vital for successful risk management, providing a competitive advantage by reducing uncertainty and increasing opportunities for success.

Achieve your customers' expectations

Meeting customer expectations is a key goal of information security programs, crucial for maintaining business viability and trust. A breach, leading to abnormal customer churn, can result in significant losses. Confidentiality involves protecting customer information, integrity ensures data remains uncorrupted, and availability guarantees timely access to products and services. NotPetya's impact on FedEx/TNT exemplifies the potential fallout, causing massive operational disruptions and substantial customer losses. Companies must uphold promises made in contracts, be they standardized or negotiated individually. Activities include reviewing contracts, integrating security requirements into daily operations, and promptly notifying customers if commitments are not met. While notification may seem risky, the consequences of violating customer trust are far greater if issues are left unaddressed.

Cyberattack and failure resilience

Cyber resilience, a key goal in cybersecurity programs, is vital to withstand the potential severe damage or business closure resulting from cyber-attacks. Cases like Colorado Timberline's shutdown due to ransomware and Norsk Hydro's significant financial losses illustrate the risks. Maersk's recovery from the NonPetya attack, Sony Pictures' data breach consequences, and Mossack Fonseca's closure due to the Panama Papers reveal the varied impacts. Stuxnet's sabotage of Iran's Natanz plant emphasizes the national-level implications. The insidious nature of integrity attacks highlights potential dangers in sectors like healthcare. Strengthening resilience against cyber threats is paramount for organizational survival.

Compliance with laws and regulations

Ensuring compliance with applicable laws and regulations is a major goal of information security programs. Given the rising significance of cybersecurity, an increasing number of laws and regulations are expected. These cover various governance levels, from multinational to national, state, and local, with some industries practicing self-regulation. Notable examples include the Sarbanes-Oxley Act for publicly traded US companies, Payment Card Industry Data Security Standard (PCIDSS) for credit card data protection, and data breach notification laws at state and EU levels. Industry-specific regulations like the Federal Information Security Management Act (FISMA) and Health Insurance Portability and Accountability Act (HIPAA) also play a crucial role. Internationally, the General Data Protection Regulation (GDPR) and, at the US state level, the Privacy Rights Act of 2020, exemplify the growing emphasis on data privacy. Identifying and complying with relevant laws necessitates thorough research and legal guidance for confidence and effectiveness.

Executive and Board of Directors (BOD) support

Supporting executives and the board is a key goal of an information security program, focusing on three crucial areas: corporate governance, risk management, and compliance. Corporate governance involves rules to dictate corporate behavior and balance stakeholder interests. Risk management addresses high-level risk in strategic, operational, financial, and compliance aspects. Compliance ensures adherence to industry regulations and government legislation. It's essential to differentiate between compliance and security, recognizing compliance as meeting specific requirements at a given moment. Due care, an informal part of GRC (Governance, Risk Management, and Compliance), is crucial for legal protection against negligence claims. Comparing security practices with similar organizations and accessing independent information sources is vital. The information security program should convey goals, progress, and future plans to the board, facilitating informed decision-making with easily understandable data.

Essential functions of a program

An information security program encompasses various functions, often handled by distinct teams or outsourced in smaller organizations. The Security Operations Center (SOC) is a key component, monitoring and defending information systems, typically supported by a Security Information and Event Management (SIEM) system. SOC staff includes analysts, security engineers, and managers with relevant credentials. Strategic business planning involves aligning new technologies with risk tolerance, creating multi-year roadmaps. Cybersecurity guidance is provided for significant projects like software migrations or implementing cloud services. Information security teams may support compliance activities, particularly during audits. Administrative functions cover identity and access management, vendor evaluations, and firewall administration. Risk management, dealing with uncertainty, is embedded across all information security functions and addressed annually.

Determine your role

As the leader of the new information security program, you hold unique responsibilities that cannot be delegated. Creating a program vision is crucial, serving as the foundation for emotional engagement, shaping the organizational culture, and setting performance expectations. A compelling vision fosters motivation for your staff to achieve ambitious goals. Without a program vision, connecting with the program becomes challenging, leading to disengagement. Collaborating with team members and stakeholders, we formulated a bold purpose statement: "Peace of mind is our profession." This statement aligned our program with the larger organization, emphasizing the parallels between insurance and information security. From this purpose, performance expectations were established for individuals and the team.

We focused on viewing ourselves as insurance professionals, promoting education through internal classes, and fostering diversity to enhance problem-solving capabilities. Embracing differences required emotional maturity and strong leadership to avoid dysfunction. Additionally, setting high-level program goals is a unique responsibility. These goals articulate how the program contributes to the organization's success and guide the organization of people, processes, technologies, and management. At the insurance company, our program goals included supporting business strategy, protecting critical information, ensuring compliance, maintaining trusted relationships, enhancing competitive position, and promoting information security education. While vision, cultural requirements, and top-level expectations cannot be delegated, the rest of the workload should be delegated to empower staff growth. Delegating responsibilities might be challenging but is essential for staff development, and seeking guidance from a supervisor or mentor can help improve delegation skills.

Build a team

To build an effective team for your program, carefully identify necessary activities and their frequency based on program goals, organizational policies, and cultural considerations. Assess budget constraints and staffing limits. Differentiate core program activities from those that can be delegated. For core activities, create position descriptions and hire accordingly, prioritizing based on core competencies. When changing duties for an inherited staff, proceed cautiously, ensuring a fit between duties, attitudes, skills, and personalities. Be mindful of hiring individuals whose energy preferences align with the nature of their roles. Consider hiring for attitude and training for skill, emphasizing aptitude for technical roles. Administer aptitude tests for candidates, especially if transitioning from another department. For delegated activities, create statements of work with measurable outcomes and prioritize finding competent vendors through collaboration with supervisors, peers, and contracts department.

The need for management

For a long time, there has been a debate about whether organizations need more leaders or managers. However, it's a trick question, as both are essential. John Kotter, a leadership expert, emphasizes that leadership aims at producing useful change, while management is about maintaining reliable and efficient operations. Effective management is crucial for upholding the status quo and ensuring the confidentiality, integrity, and availability of organizational information. Examples of good management practices include reporting program status to senior managers, holding staff accountable for delegated work, processing access control requests accurately and promptly, and reviewing violation reports to detect and stop online misconduct. While management tools come naturally to some, mastering leadership tools can be more challenging, leading to potential mistakes.

The need for leadership

John Kotter, a renowned leadership expert and former Harvard Business School professor, defines leadership as involving vision, people engagement, empowerment, and, most importantly, producing meaningful change. In contrast, management, according to Kotter, revolves around maintaining the status quo, akin to hitting the bullseye in a game. For an information security program implementer, leadership skills are crucial when influencing organizational members to adopt better cybersecurity practices. Engaging people with a compelling vision and maintaining their enthusiasm is key to achieving consistently positive outcomes and reducing unplanned turnover.

Leadership in this context involves navigating human emotions, necessitating empathy, strong interpersonal communication, boundary-setting, and likability. Research suggests that balancing warmth with competence is essential for being highly influential. Building and maintaining relationships through emotionally intelligent interactions enhances influence. While management skills are vital, a successful implementer must possess a nuanced blend of management and leadership capabilities, switching between them as needed. Developing leadership skills involves training, experiential learning, stepping out of one's comfort zone, seeking guidance from admired leaders, embracing failure constructively, and enhancing self-awareness through tools like DISC or 360-degree feedback surveys.

Sources of controls

Let's explore specific sources for information security controls, essential for meeting program goals and managing risk. While compliance mandates like Sarbanes-Oxley (SOX) provide guidelines, their focus is narrow, often lacking detailed implementation steps. In contrast, standards like Payment Card Industry Data Security Standard (PCI DSS) offer specific measures for protecting credit card data. However, neither should be the primary source for controls due to their limited scope.

More comprehensive sources include widely-used information security standards. COBIT (Control Objectives for Information Technologies) by ISACA is business-oriented, suitable for larger companies but might be complex. NIST

Special Publication 800-53 targets US federal information systems, offering extensive controls but may be challenging for smaller organizations. ISO 27002 is an international standard for global businesses, providing a catalog of controls and implementation guidance, requiring a license.

Consensus standards, involving multiple stakeholders, are also valuable. The Critical Security Controls for Effective Cyber Defense by the Center for Internet Security comprises 20 highly effective controls against cyber-attacks, yet is primarily technical and costly. The NIST Cybersecurity Framework offers governance for private sector organizations to enhance cyber resilience, though measuring implementation success is challenging.

Each of these sources has distinct advantages and limitations, and the choice depends on factors like organizational size, global presence, and specific business needs.

Organize around cyber resilience

Ensuring resilience to cyber-attacks and failures is a primary goal of an information security program. To achieve this, we prioritize resilience by selecting a high-level framework, choosing controls that explicitly support cyber resilience, satisfying customer requirements, compliance mandates, and supporting executives. The implementation and measurement of these controls form the basis for our cyber risk management program. Two frameworks, the NIST Cybersecurity Framework and Gartner's model, share similarities in identifying, protecting, detecting, responding, and recovering from cybersecurity events. While Gartner's model emphasizes prediction, prevention, detection, response, and recovery, adopting the NIST framework, with its 98 controls, offers a comprehensive approach without the need for a Gartner subscription. The NIST framework also includes a crosswalk that correlates Cybersecurity Framework outcomes with specific ISO 27001 controls, facilitating ISO 27001 compliance if desired.

Information security program design

After exploring five key sources of information security controls and emphasizing the importance of cyber resilience, the next step is to select controls for effective program implementation. To optimize efficiency, choose a unified set of controls aligning with program goals, ensuring workforce adherence, managing risk, and demonstrating compliance. While compliance pressures are significant, creating a single internal program covering all mandates avoids duplication and reduces costs. Utilize a comprehensive policy-driven structure, where policies influence standards, processes, and procedures. This approach enhances risk management, cost-effectiveness, competitive advantage, and facilitates compliance with new mandates. When faced with conflicting mandates, prioritize the most restrictive to address real risks effectively. Regularly review and update your program design annually to align with evolving business needs and changing requirements.

Communicate with executives

Meet your boss and executives' communication needs by regularly providing updates on the current status of your four goals: meeting customer expectations, being cyber resilient, being compliant, and supporting executives. Understand their preferred communication style, whether it's through discussions or written reports, and align your approach accordingly. When addressing decision-making, define problems using language they understand, present three or four summarized options ranging from conservative to aggressive solutions, and emphasize costs and benefits. Ensure you don't make decisions unless explicitly delegated. For storytelling, utilize a scorecard for a 15-minute overview. Present the summary scorecard, highlight top strengths, move to the graphical version, discuss the top five risks briefly, and spend time on the project portfolio visualizer to showcase efforts in closing gaps. Adapt and seek feedback to refine your communication strategies.

Communicate with stakeholders

Effectively communicate information security to various stakeholders by understanding their preferences and using existing communication channels. Learn from experienced individuals and leverage organizational change management experts. In larger organizations, use multiple channels, such as email and video, to broadcast messages to reach a broader audience. Request to join regular staff meetings with supervisors to present information and ensure their support. Gain the support of supervisors' managers first and provide them with advance notice of your messages. Be prepared for planning and address objections while maintaining progress. Secure the support of peers through collaboration and adapt your approach based on organizational culture. Seek mentorship for strategy development. When dealing with customers or the media, involve the public relations or corporate communications team for guidance.

Communicate with auditors

Working with auditors may seem daunting, but it doesn't have to be. Auditors aim to enhance organizational performance by improving risk management, control, and governance processes. They can be internal or external, with internal auditors likely familiar with your company culture, and external auditors reporting to an outside entity. Typically, auditors review policies, management reports, and conduct control testing. Expect written questions about controls, and respond within the specified timeframe. Maintain respect and friendliness with auditors, but don't take orders as if they were your boss. It's crucial to respectfully disagree and push back when necessary. Auditors may struggle with interpreting regulations within your operational context. If there's a disagreement, seek advice from your boss, assertively present your compliance reasons, and submit a thoughtful management response if necessary. Confidence and respect can go a long way in navigating the audit process.

Construct an annual program of work

To enhance the effectiveness of your information security program, establish an annual program of work. This calendar-driven approach integrates three key workflows: preparing for annual budgeting, conducting annual risk management activities, and reporting progress on top risks. The events in these workflows, occurring once or three times a year, align with specific months. Begin in September with a review of your program's structure and a tri-annual update to your cybersecurity scorecard. October involves publishing the scorecard and reviewing processes for measuring information risks. November focuses on processes for understanding information risks, while December involves managing information risks. In January, perform a tri-annual scorecard update and initiate annual risk measurements. February entails publishing the tri-annual scorecard and continuing risk measurements. March completes the annual risk measurements, followed by April's analysis of the new risk posture. May includes a tri-annual scorecard update and preparing annual proposals based on risk measurements. In June, communicate the scorecard update and gain support for risk management proposals. July involves creating annual budget requests, and in August, take a break.

DATA SECURITY POLICY

1. SCOPE; DEFINITIONS

1.1 This Security Policy pertains to Supplier's activities under the Agreement and the handling of ABC Inc. Information.

1.2 Definitions:

1.2.1 "Anonymize" means processing data, including ABC Inc. Information, to prevent user or source identification.

1.2.2 "ABC Inc. Information" includes all data acquired, accessed, or maintained by Supplier related to the Agreement.

2. ABC INC. SECURITY POLICY

2.1 Basic Security Requirements:

2.1.1 Firewall: Maintain a network firewall to protect ABC Inc. Information accessible via the Internet.

2.1.2 Updates: Keep systems and software up-to-date to ensure security of ABC Inc. Information.

2.1.3 Antimalware: Utilize and update antimalware software to mitigate threats.

2.1.4 Encryption: Encrypt data at rest and during transmission following industry best practices.

2.1.5 Testing: Regularly test security systems and processes to meet Security Policy requirements.

2.1.6 Remote Access: Implement multifactor authentication for external access to systems holding ABC Inc. Information.

2.2 Forensic Destruction: Ensure complete forensic destruction of hardware, software, or media containing ABC Inc. Information before disposal.

2.3 Security Review:

2.3.1 ABC Inc. may request Supplier to complete risk assessments periodically.

2.3.2 Other Reviews: ABC Inc. may review Supplier's systems processing ABC Inc. Information, with Supplier's cooperation.

2.3.3 Remediation: If deficiencies are identified, Supplier will remedy them at its own cost within an agreed timeframe.

Chapter 3 Leveraging Security Metrics in Your Organization

Cybersecurity is hard to measure

Successful businesses rely on metrics to guide action plans and achieve objectives. While standard metrics are easily defined for businesses focused on selling products or services, cybersecurity lacks similarly well-defined metrics. Unlike concrete units like dollars and customer numbers used in business metrics, cybersecurity deals with the more challenging task of measuring risk. Unlike business metrics that aim for more customers and lower acquisition costs, cybersecurity controls come with a cost, introducing complexity. In the realm of cybersecurity, various factors influence decision-making, such as an organization's inability to update software due to a lack of system inventory or concerns about system disruption during updates. Each organization may choose different approaches, making it challenging to measure such cybersecurity decisions effectively.

Cybersecurity investment

Cybersecurity investment typically involves head count, salaries, consultants, and expenses, competing for budget allocation in organizations. Unlike revenue-generating departments, the security team's impact on revenue is less direct, focusing on protecting value. The decision to add head count to the security team requires assessing the value being protected. Cybersecurity involves uncertainties, and risk tolerance becomes a crucial concept in determining the appropriate investment level. Organizations, like individuals, have varying risk tolerances, influenced by factors like industry, regulatory environment, and organizational maturity. Identifying and understanding an organization's risk tolerance is a continuous, structured process facilitated through discussions in board or committee meetings. In these discussions, the chief information security officer plays a crucial role in outlining cybersecurity risks and proposing strategies, with security metrics aiding in these conversations.

Define success for a cybersecurity program

In the information security industry, protecting value is the core objective of a cybersecurity program. Security leaders should prioritize understanding how the organization creates and retains value. Instead of comparing activities to security best practices, focus on demonstrating objectives and results to stakeholders. Communicate the value of security work consistently to relevant stakeholders, as passionate dedication alone may not secure necessary budgets. Share information regularly to build awareness and promote the security program, emphasizing the positive impact on the company's risk posture. Prioritize transparency over secrecy in sharing security data, ensuring protection of sensitive information.

Cybersecurity program maturity

Cybersecurity programs, based on their maturity levels, require different metrics, with one key benefit being increased visibility. The desired direction for vulnerability count depends on program maturity. In a mature program with established defect discovery methods, a consistent tracking process, and stable procedures, decreasing vulnerability count over time is ideal. However, in less mature programs introducing new defect discovery methods, an increase in vulnerability count during the establishment phase is expected. For programs with no defect discovery mechanisms, the desired direction is to increase vulnerability count, emphasizing the importance of detection capabilities. The assumption is that technology is inherently vulnerable, and program maturity influences the ability to detect existing vulnerabilities. While the instinct is to consider fewer vulnerabilities as better, it's crucial to distinguish between actual vulnerabilities and known vulnerabilities. Cybersecurity leaders should grasp and effectively convey this nuance when presenting vulnerability metrics to stakeholders.

The executive mindset

Cybersecurity practitioners often face challenges in communicating with company executives, leading to a perceived disconnect. This arises from the lack of effective security metrics, hindering a shared understanding of cybersecurity's value. To bridge this gap, practitioners should approach executives with curiosity, recognizing their intelligence and strategic capabilities. Executives may rely on media for cybersecurity information, and practitioners must connect incidents to organizational impact, prevention strategies, and relevant frameworks. Avoid framing cybersecurity investment solely in financial terms if it's not your strength, as it can lead to unproductive discussions. Instead, focus on clear communication and understanding the company's long-term strategy to align cybersecurity plans effectively.

The business mindset

Discussing the go-to-market strategy for an organization, I'll focus on marketing and sales leadership perspectives and how cybersecurity professionals can enhance communication with these functions. In marketing, responsible for the organization's message and brand, engaging early and often with marketing teams can help cybersecurity professionals stay ahead of third-party vendor engagements, facilitating proactive collaboration. Additionally, partnering with marketing on privacy initiatives, especially regarding prospect outreach, provides an opportunity for cybersecurity to offer valuable perspectives. Moving to sales, understanding their goal to close deals allows cybersecurity professionals to leverage vendor security assessments from the other side of the table. Establishing relationships with sales leadership helps address hurdles like vendor-security assessments, ensuring alignment with buyer expectations on security and compliance frameworks. Regular check-ins with sales leadership enable tracking and adapting to customer requests for specific compliance standards, enhancing the organization's overall security posture.

The technical leadership mindset

Contrary to common belief, cybersecurity isn't solely the responsibility of security professionals; it involves collaboration across various individuals, including engineers and technical leaders responsible for building and protecting technology. Engineers value efficiency, take pride in their work, and prefer figuring things out independently. When partnering with engineering teams, it's essential to respect their autonomy and focus on conveying the "why" and "what" of cybersecurity initiatives, allowing engineers to contribute their expertise on the "how." Engaging them for input on security decisions, sharing requirements, and asking about implementation methods fosters collaboration and efficiency. Building trusted relationships with engineering leaders involves understanding their priorities, measuring team performance, and offering assistance based on their needs. It's crucial to address security concerns collaboratively, involving engineers in decision-making and proactively managing technical debt to enhance overall cybersecurity efforts.

Defining a risk management objective

After understanding your organization's value creation, proposing a cybersecurity strategy involves presenting a plan and budget. Key considerations include:

1. Use cybersecurity as a competitive differentiator:

   - Evaluate customer expectations regarding security.

   - Assess if security can set your product apart.

   - Emphasize strong security as a competitive advantage.

2. Comply with regulatory requirements, contracts, or standards:

   - Identify applicable security-related requirements.

   - Leverage compliance as a motivator for the security plan.

3. Achieve a defensible level of due care:

   - Define due care in your business context.

   - Promote strong security practices based on due care expectations.

4. Prevent recurring cybersecurity problems:

   - Assess maturity in identifying and addressing similar issues.

   - Use reliable defect discovery processes for consistent improvement.

5. Reduce the probability of disrupting critical systems:

   - Identify and list critical assets for effective security management.

   - Implement defect discovery processes for critical assets.

6. Require fixes for well-known attack vulnerabilities:

   - Categorize security flaws by exploit ease.

   - Utilize tracking and reporting for timely bug fixes.

7. Achieve comparable cybersecurity to peers or competition:

   - Focus on competitive analysis in your company's strategy.

- Gather benchmarking data to support cybersecurity investment decisions.

This Risk Management Objectives approach addresses specific questions to align cybersecurity strategies with business operations and security posture. These objectives guide the development of a comprehensive cybersecurity strategy, plan, and budget.

How to use a risk management objective

For a detailed example of implementing a risk management objective, let's consider objective number five: reducing the probability of malicious attackers halting critical systems and applications. This approach demonstrates an understanding of business operations, fostering trust and obtaining stakeholder buy-in.

1. Identify Critical Systems:

   - Compile a comprehensive inventory of critical systems, applications, and their respective owners.

2. Security Testing:

   - Conduct thorough security testing on each critical component, employing a defense-in-depth strategy.

3. Investment for Security Testing:

   - If security testing is lacking, allocate additional resources for this crucial step.

4. Vulnerability Ranking:

   - Assess vulnerabilities in each component and rank them based on severity.

5. Research on Exploitation:

   - Investigate recent attacks on similar systems to understand potential exploitation methods and impact.

6. Collaboration with Owners:

   - Collaborate with business and technical owners to share findings and jointly address identified vulnerabilities.

Implementing this process not only strengthens security measures but also involves stakeholders in a collaborative effort to safeguard critical systems.

Examples of risk management objectives

A risk management objective is a goal outlining the desired state for risk management. In the context of businesses relying on software, proactive cybersecurity investment is crucial to mitigate risks such as malicious attacks and data breaches. Defining a specific risk management objective aligns stakeholders, facilitating agreement on the investment needed for the cybersecurity program. Without clear objectives, justifying cybersecurity investments may face challenges, as seen in the analogy of considering costly window replacements for an old house. The lack of defined risk management objectives can lead to uncertainty about the team's focus and effectiveness, emphasizing the importance of clear goals agreed upon by executive management.

Incidents detected internally vs. externally

To effectively communicate security metrics, relying on a single number lacks meaningful context. For instance, the number of security incidents alone, such as five or a hundred, doesn't convey the necessary information. Utilizing ratios involving two or more numbers provides a more insightful perspective on how the actual measurement compares to intended or planned outcomes. In the context of security incidents, the industry's mindset has shifted from trying to prevent incidents altogether to recognizing that they are inevitable. Instead of merely reporting the number of incidents, a more valuable metric is the percentage of incidents detected internally versus externally. This metric reflects visibility and progress in security response, with the calculation involving dividing the number of incidents detected internally by those detected externally. Adjusting the plan or goal percentage based on the security program's maturity enhances the effectiveness of this metric.

Fixes implemented within SLA

Various methods can uncover security vulnerabilities, such as static or dynamic scanning, pen tests, or third-party reports. Addressing vulnerabilities is crucial, but their severity varies from critical to low, assessed by the Common Vulnerability Scoring System (CVSS). Critical issues demand immediate fixes, while less severe ones may have more extended timelines based on organizational risk tolerance. A useful metric for vulnerability management is the percentage of fixes within the Service Level Agreement (SLA). For instance, if 70% of vulnerabilities were remediated within SLA, it indicates program effectiveness compared to planned goals. Focusing on critical and high severity vulnerabilities can provide a more specific metric, such as 100% remediation within SLA for these high-risk issues.

Apply security metrics

Unlike being a mere supplement or fix, security is more akin to a dance—a dynamic interplay shaped by numerous decisions and actions. Security metrics aim not to impose order on chaos but to acknowledge the inherent truth and the continuous evolution essential to cybersecurity programs.

Chapter 4 Influencing the Board and C-Suite for a CISO

Navigating your executive relationships

For new CISOs or cyber leaders, emphasizing resources and budget alone may not guarantee success. The people factor is a crucial key for executing any strategy effectively. A successful leader needs a deep understanding of managing people at various levels, including executives, peers, and subordinates. Recognizing the operational methods of executives enables effective navigation and collaboration for meaningful outcomes. We will explore the perspectives of key leaders, such as the CEO, CFO, CRO, and CIO, along with discussing the role of the boardroom and shaping organizational culture. To enhance interaction with executive leaders, adopting a business-oriented communication style without excessive technical jargon is essential.

The lens of the four birds

Understanding the reasons behind human actions and communication styles is crucial for building effective collaborative relationships. A CISO leader, tasked with influencing and implementing changes, benefits from comprehending the motivations and personalities of various executive leaders. The DOPE personality test, categorizing individuals into four birds (Dove, Eagle, Owl, and Peacock), provides a simple yet insightful approach. Doves are peace-oriented team players but avoid confrontation. Eagles are bold, decisive, and thrive on challenges, though their directness can be misinterpreted. Owls are wise, logical, and detail-oriented, while peacocks are enthusiastic, talkative, and optimistic. Utilizing these personality insights enhances communication effectiveness with different stakeholders, a valuable asset for engaging with executive leaders.

Starting with the biggest executive: Your CEO

The Chief Executive Officer (CEO) holds the highest position in a company, overseeing its overall success, vision, mission, and strategy. A Harvard study tracking 27 CEOs revealed that CEOs spend their time diversely, with 21% on strategy, 25% on reviews, 25% on people and relationships, and 16% on organization and culture. CEOs answer to the board of directors, responsible for the company's sustainability and profitability. CEOs are the public faces of the company, appearing at events, engaging in speaking roles, and addressing cyber risk concerns. As cyber-attacks increase, CEOs are expected to be accountable for data breaches, emphasizing the need for their active involvement in addressing cyber risks.

Winning over the CEO in your cyber resilience mission

To win your CEO over as a cyber advocate, it's crucial to establish a partnership and demonstrate that managing cyber risks aligns with their business goals. CEOs may assume cyber risks are delegated to experts, but history shows they are personally held accountable in a crisis. Establishing this alliance early in your relationship is key. Communicate the business impact of cyber risks, emphasizing its connection to enterprise risk management. Highlight how a robust cyber resilience strategy contributes to the CEO's goals, ensuring company performance, reputation, and shareholder returns. Emphasize that poor cybersecurity posture can lead to disruptions, financial losses, reputation damage, and a decline in customer trust. Stress the importance of CEO commitment and support in facing cyber threats proactively. Acknowledge that cyber incidents are inevitable, but diligent preparation and commitment can significantly mitigate their impact.

Partnering with your CEO in their first 30 days

To effect real change within the organization, it's essential to focus on cybersecurity culture. While the CSO or cyber leader plays a crucial role in shaping the cybersecurity strategy, creating a culture of cybersecurity requires collective effort. All employees should grasp security fundamentals beyond policy compliance. Senior management, including the CEO, must lead by example. Despite other pressing concerns for CEOs, cybersecurity should not be neglected, as threat actors do not wait for readiness. New leadership changes or mergers and acquisitions can be targeted, emphasizing the need for proactive security measures. Building cyber resilience involves intentional culture development, aligning with CEOs to accelerate growth. Establishing a trusted relationship with CEOs, showing understanding of their vision and goals, and collaborating on solutions will make them see the benefits of partnering with security leaders.

Understanding the CFO

Meet the Chief Financial Officer (CFO), the top financial professional in an organization. The CFO handles tasks such as tracking cash flow, financial planning, budget creation, and analyzing the company's financial status. Traditionally, CFOs act as financial controllers, focusing on transaction details. However, modern CFOs are forward-thinking, driving strategy and emphasizing the narrative behind the numbers. While the CEO sets direction and culture, the CFO is the change agent, implementing culture and preparing the budget. Visionary CFOs look to the future, collaborating closely with leadership and offering strategic recommendations. Understanding CFOs is crucial as cybersecurity ranks among the top five risks, and CFOs play a key role in managing this risk within enterprise risk management. CFOs assess the broad and long-term financial impact of a cyber-attack, considering reputational, regulatory, and share price implications. A strong cyber posture, if well-executed, can support organizational growth goals and enhance overall business strength, fostering employee confidence and performance. In the upcoming segment, we will explore aligning cyber risk priorities with the CFO's key concerns.

Aligning cyber risk with the CFO role

Now that we understand the CFO's role better, let's examine our key priorities and their connection to the impact of a cyber-attack. In the realm of finance, cybercrimes like phishing, social engineering, and business email compromise (BEC) pose significant threats. BEC schemes, identified as the costliest cybercrimes, incurred losses of around $2.4 billion in 2022, according to the FBI's Internet Crime Complaint Center. For instance, an employee processing a fraudulent vendor invoice can result in substantial financial misdirection. Social engineering attacks targeting finance executives, such as the London Blue hacker group's actions, demonstrate the rise in these cybercrimes. CFOs, despite their financial acumen, are susceptible to such scams.

Another pertinent issue for CFOs is cyber insurance. In the past decade, insurers increasingly inquire about a company's cybersecurity measures and offer cyber insurance as a risk transfer option. This shift has led CFOs to correlate cyber-attack frequency and costs with insurance premiums, impacting their perception of cyber risk. CFOs comprehend financial costs due to cyber-attacks and data breaches, including immediate expenses like penalties, fines, and notification costs. Additional costs may stem from forensic investigations, compensatory actions, procedural changes, security enhancements, or compensation for losses. In successfully communicating with CFOs, it is crucial to articulate the broader business impact, encompassing disruptions to core systems, potential business paralysis, third-party costs, legal expenses, brand damage, customer losses, sales reductions, profit declines, market share valuation drops, and IPO delays. Focusing on the business impact can reshape their cybersecurity mindset and emphasize the importance of resilience.

Changing mindsets on costs and budgets

We've extensively explored aligning cyber needs with the CFO's motivations, emphasizing the need for a mindset shift. Rather than viewing cyber risk as an additional cost, it should be seen as a necessary investment. The shift involves focusing on Return on Value (ROV) or Return on Objective (ROO), akin to a nation's defense strategy, preparing for potential cyber threats. Benchmarking against peer companies' cyber resilience is another approach to gauge the effectiveness of cybersecurity investments.

Investments in regulatory compliance, such as GDPR and PCI DSS, contribute to building a credible cyber program. The CFO's quantitative approach is valuable for analyzing cyber risk, emphasizing the need for quantification over qualitative methods traditionally used by cybersecurity professionals. Lead and lag indicators, including financial fines and incident response costs, assist in assessing cybersecurity threats and needs. The Finance team, leveraging risk quantification, plays a crucial role in aligning cybersecurity strategies with business goals.

In modern CFO roles, using numbers to inspire change aids prioritization and effective cyber risk management as part of Enterprise Risk Management (ERM). Risk transference, focusing on valuable data, becomes essential for efficient business decisions, with cybersecurity being a crucial aspect.

The focus areas that are important to your CRO

The Chief Risk Officer (CRO), a senior executive, oversees the identification and assessment of business risks impacting profitability and productivity. The CRO champions Enterprise Risk Management (ERM) and addresses evolving cyber threats. While ISO 31000 is the standard for risk management, ISO 27005 focuses more on cyber risk. CROs prioritize safety, resilience, customer commitments, and regulatory compliance. Anticipating complex risks, they analyze historical data to predict the future, ensuring the organization can respond effectively within a changing risk profile. Assessing intangible technology risks poses challenges, hindering ERM strategies and board support. The CRO adds value by facilitating risk-informed decisions and aligning cybersecurity risk management with business operations.

Connecting the dots with how CROs perceive risks

To effectively combat cyber risk, collaboration between the Chief Risk Officer (CRO) and the Chief Information Security Officer (CISO) is crucial. Both teams should work together to categorize, identify, and quantify cyber risks. This collaboration extends to physical security, health and safety, data governance, and other relevant teams. The CRO and CISO align on frameworks, operating models, reporting, and incident management. The CISO manages mitigation controls and compliance for digital risk, ensuring alignment with the organization's risk tolerance. The CRO, supported by the CISO, facilitates discussions on cyber risk management, encouraging board-level engagement. When communicating with the CRO, emphasize cyber risk within the context of business risk and enterprise risk management. For effective engagement, focus on demonstrating the impact of cyber events on business activities, aligning with the CRO's key priorities. Consider how your current cyber risk concerns can be articulated to resonate with the CRO's focus areas, emphasizing understanding their motivations for better communication.

Cyber and risk: The power duo and trigger questions

In cybersecurity, collaboration between the Chief Risk Officer (CRO) and the Chief Information Security Officer (CISO) is crucial for a balanced risk posture. Together, they can create structured scenarios to quantify the severity of cyber events, providing valuable reporting to the board. When engaging with the CRO, ask about their understanding of cyber risk, its integration into the Enterprise Risk Management (ERM) strategy, and the metrics used to assess the cyber risk profile. Inquire about the evolving focus on cyber threats, future predictions, and how cyber risk tolerance aligns with other risks. Close collaboration with the CRO can yield meaningful business outcomes and enhance the perception of cyber risk within the organization.

Meeting the CIO: Welcome to their world

The Chief Information Officer (CIO) oversees IT strategies in a company, with key priorities in 2022 including hybrid work infrastructure (61%), cybersecurity (52%), and digital enablement (46%), according to Gartner Peer Insights. Beyond day-to-day IT management, a proficient CIO aligns technology with long-term business goals. Balancing business drivers, security risks, and financial considerations is crucial, considering factors like on-premises solutions and operational expenditure. Expecting the CIO to possess a comprehensive knowledge of cybersecurity, like the CFO and CRO, is unrealistic, emphasizing the need for advocacy and empowerment in this specialized area.

Innovation and technology: What's the conflict with cyber?

Historically, roles in information security have originated from the IT discipline. A 2021 ISACA survey showed 48% of security teams report to a CISO, while 25% report to the CIO. Another survey by Heidrick & Struggles in 2022 found that 48% of CISOs report to the CIO. Experiences with CIOs vary; some see conflicts of interest, with CIOs withholding cyber risk information or prioritizing legacy systems over security, impacting revenue. The CIO often focuses on driving business value through technology, while the CISO specializes in information security management. Despite differences, effective collaboration between the CIO and CISO is crucial for finding a balance between cyber risk, business operations, and revenue, emphasizing the importance of strong communication and collaboration on cybersecurity strategy.

Building friendships and getting their critical support

If you're new to the company or need to establish a relationship with your CIO, start with an open and friendly conversation. Understand their strategy and goals, and determine if they see cybersecurity as a business or IT risk. Use analogies to convey that, like brakes in a car, security isn't a showstopper but a necessary component for acceleration. Collaborate with your CIO on cyber risk concerns, especially before significant programs like digital transformations. Emphasize being an ally who helps with solutions, applying a cyber risk lens. As trust builds, CIOs will initiate cybersecurity discussions, viewing you as a subject matter expert and trusted partner in achieving secure goals.

Six guidelines for your board

When addressing the board about cyber risk, simplicity and clarity are key. Board directors often desire straightforward communication without technical jargon. Instead of presenting random numbers, focus on explaining how one risk, including cyber risk, impacts another. The CISO should not only highlight the interconnectedness of cyber risk but also showcase the success of mitigation measures. This helps the board prioritize expenditures, assess return on investments, and recognize the value the CISO brings to the organization. Guidelines for framing cyber risk to the board include emphasizing their joint responsibility with C-Suite executives, assessing cybersecurity investments, understanding exposure, considering risk transfer options, staying informed about regulatory changes, and fostering collaboration within the industry and information sharing organizations for cyber resilience.

Your role in shaping the organization's culture

Your role in fostering a secure culture is pivotal. Cultures are often taken for granted, but they significantly influence everything we do. Addressing poor security culture is integral to our cybersecurity strategy, and building it starts with people. Leaders should not accept the cultural status quo; instead, they can recruit champions or advocates to influence the organization positively. Spending time understanding business stakeholders and turning them into advocates is crucial. Regular engagement with C-Suite Executives can provide diverse perspectives. Varying training methods, such as gamification, helps engage and retain a security mindset. The ultimate goal is a sustainable, transformative security culture within a healthy organizational culture. Trust, a safe space for innovation, and honesty are essential for a positive security culture. Success in culture change requires collaboration from top executives to middle management, emphasizing that building cyber resilience is a collective effort.

Chapter 5 Cybersecurity Vendor Selection and Management

What is outsourcing?

Outsourcing, derived from "outside resourcing," is a term with varied perceptions. While it can carry a negative connotation in the US, it presents a positive opportunity elsewhere globally. Setting aside these connotations, let's focus on practical aspects. The Economist notes outsourcing's presence since World War II, evolving to include business processes, public services, offshoring, nearshoring, and even cooperative sourcing. The global market for business process outsourcing is projected to surpass $343 billion by 2025 according to Forrester Research.

Why outsource?

Organizations often outsource work for various reasons. For instance, Apple designs its iPhones in-house but outsources assembly to companies like Foxconn in China, aligning with Peter Drucker's advice to "Do what you do best and outsource the rest." Outsourcing motives also include lowering taxes, evading government regulations, and reducing business expenses, with cost reduction being a common objective. However, Drucker's concept emphasizes organizational effectiveness by focusing on core identity. Despite the benefits, outsourcing may not always deliver as expected due to hidden costs, such as vendor selection expenses (up to 2% of the deal value), substantial transition costs, parallel work with employees, layoff expenses, communication challenges, cultural barriers, and potential high turnover in offshore teams, causing delays in the transition process.

Why outsource cybersecurity?

Outsourcing cybersecurity can initially appear as either favorable or unfavorable. However, it boils down to a matter of trust. Simply outsourcing tedious or costly cybersecurity tasks while keeping more engaging responsibilities for the internal team may not be the optimal approach, as outsourcing decisions should consider trust implications. Despite building a rational business case, strategic and cultural dimensions make outsourcing cybersecurity unsuitable for everyone. Factors such as a unique and hard-to-understand internal culture or highly valuable trade secrets may hinder outsourcing suitability. Considering these factors is crucial when contemplating cybersecurity outsourcing. As mentioned earlier, alongside cost reduction, outsourcing aims to enhance effectiveness by allowing organizations to leverage their strengths. Outsourcing emerges as a solution to offload the complexities of staff acquisition and retention to specialized organizations.

What are the benefits of outsourcing?

Outsourcing can provide financial, focus, and scale benefits. Financially, it can lead to decreased operating costs, as vendors bring their tools and infrastructure, eliminating the need for capital expenditure. Additionally, outsourcing allows organizations to shift from fixed to variable costs, making them easier to manage. In terms of focus, outsourcing enhances decision-making quality by leveraging the vendor's perspective and security expertise. It also enables the organization's cybersecurity team to concentrate on core functions, such as policy setting, architecture, design, and risk management. The third major benefit is scalability, allowing organizations to quickly adjust their cybersecurity capabilities based on needs. Similar to cloud computing's flexibility in adding resources, outsourcing cybersecurity enables rapid scaling up or down. For instance, during a cyber-attack, increased security events can be efficiently managed with on-demand storage from a vendor, preserving valuable records.

How is managing outsourced work different from managing staff?

We'll explore the distinctions in managing outsourced work versus staff, focusing on managed security service provider (MSSP). An MSSP can handle various security functions like intrusion detection system monitoring, operating a 24/7 security operations center, and conducting vulnerability testing. The two common business arrangements with MSSPs are outsourcing, where work is conducted at the MSSP offices, and co-sourcing, a blend of outsourcing and insourcing where the MSSP utilizes the organization's equipment installed in its building. A newer form of co-sourcing is Security as a Service, integrating the service provider's equipment into the organization's infrastructure with a monthly or annual subscription, as seen in security event collection and analysis. Managing insourced versus outsourced work differs in three main aspects: control, measurement, and flexibility. In insourcing, there is daily control over staff, whereas outsourcing involves greater distance and the outsourcer determining job assignments. Measurement in insourcing focuses on staff performance, while outsourcing emphasizes deliverables, such as specific times for vulnerability scans. Regarding flexibility, insourcing allows for moving staff to different tasks, while outsourcing restricts the redirection of outsourced personnel to other assignments.

What are the risks of outsourcing cybersecurity?

Outsourcing cybersecurity can fail due to two main risks: misalignment of goals and hidden costs. The first risk involves potential challenges in maintaining team morale and protecting company assets when outsourcing. Employees' morale may suffer, leading to turnover, and the contracted party might not share the same commitment during crises. Granting access to sensitive data poses security risks, and compliance obligations can be challenging, especially across international borders. The second risk, hidden costs, can undermine the outsourcing business case. These costs include layoffs, implementation delays, cultural and language inefficiencies, regulatory fines, and the possibility of the outsourcer's failure. Thorough research is essential to identify and address potential future costs.

The seven steps to successfully outsourcing cybersecurity work

When outsourcing cybersecurity tasks, it's beneficial to follow a proven seven-step process for increased success. Assuming the business case for outsourcing has been established, the steps include:

1. Identify candidate work to outsource (three broad categories).

2. Document requirements, focusing on outcomes.

3. Select a vendor, evaluating and prioritizing candidates.

4. Contract with the vendor, involving legal or contracts expertise.

5. Implement the agreement, a people-intensive step.

6. Manage the vendor, emphasizing the importance of the service level agreement.

7. Renew or possibly end the agreement.

What should you outsource?

Determining suitable tasks for outsourcing can be challenging, but a useful guideline is to retain core business tasks with employees. The work suitable for outsourcing can be categorized into three types:

1. Core Tasks: These involve high-quality decisions requiring an in-depth understanding of the business and strong relationships across the organization. Examples include chairing the Information Security Steering Committee and supporting the renewal of cybersecurity insurance policies.

2. Strategic Outsource Tasks: These tasks require research or analysis but don't demand an intricate understanding of the business. External experts assist in detailed work, enhancing the productivity of the cybersecurity team. Examples include assessing firewall effectiveness and conducting digital forensics.

3. Commodity Outsourced Tasks: Here, outsiders perform the majority of the work under direct oversight, making decisions based on pre-established rules and guidelines. Examples include resetting passwords (risky but not organization-specific) and 24/7 network security monitoring.

Examples of work to outsource

Continuous 24/7 network security monitoring poses a significant challenge for all but the largest organizations. Typically handled by a team in a Security Operation Center (SOC), maintaining reliable coverage requires eight to ten employees due to factors like sickness and training. Outsourcing SOC services is a practical option, especially as it is not a core competency for most organizations. In the U.S., hiring a Managed Security Service Provider (MSSP) for SOC services costs around $50,000 per year, compared to the higher expenses associated with an in-house cybersecurity professional, totaling almost three times the direct salary when factoring in benefits, facilities, and equipment. This cost difference presents a compelling business case for outsourcing.

However, certain tasks should not be outsourced, such as chairing the Information Security Steering Committee. This role is core to the organization's mission, involving weighty decisions that impact the entire organization. Deep knowledge of the business, risk tolerance, and successful policy operationalization, along with strong relationships with senior managers, is essential. These factors make it challenging for an outsider to effectively chair the committee, as contractors are often perceived as temporary and may not garner the necessary trust and investment from insiders.

Case study 1: Identify candidate work to outsource

As their organization expanded, the information security team recognized an increased workload. Facing resistance to adding new staff positions, they sought approval to outsource specific tasks. To initiate the process, they prepared a business case and began by categorizing tasks into core and non-core based on frequency, risk rating, and the need for in-depth understanding. Core tasks, such as project cyber risk assessments, required internal expertise due to their business-critical nature. Strategic outsourcing was applied to tasks like digital forensics, which had infrequent needs and were deemed too costly to handle in-house. Tactical outsourcing, like creating user accounts and resetting passwords, was employed for tasks with low risk, ultimately delegated to an external provider as a self-service procedure. Administrative and service account tasks, deemed riskier, were retained in-house.

Outcomes

When documenting requirements for outsourcing, focus on desired outcomes rather than monitoring the work process. Identify key metrics, such as response time for alerts or the implementation timeline for specific tasks. Consider details like the starting point for time calculations. Beyond the work itself, actively manage outcomes related to team morale, especially if layoffs are involved. Define specific goals for both departing and remaining team members. Avoid legal issues by ensuring compliance with state and federal employment laws and minimizing discrimination risks. Collaborate with HR and public affairs teams to handle potential media coverage and PR concerns associated with the outsourcing decision.

How the work gets done

While outcomes are crucial, the process matters in cybersecurity. For instance, some outsourcers may grant excessive computer permissions, violating the Principle of Least Privilege. Improper handling, like storing passwords in a help desk ticketing system, can lead to costly incidents. To address this, let the vendor establish procedures, but conduct walk-throughs to identify and rectify weaknesses. Be prepared for a potential price increase due to increased scrutiny, and conduct annual checks to ensure ongoing adherence to agreed-upon processes.

Service Level Agreements (SLA)

The service-level agreement (SLA) is vital for managing your MSSP's work and is typically a contractual document. Essential elements include detailing the service type, specifying performance levels in terms of reliability and responsiveness, outlining supervision and reporting procedures, defining incident reporting and resolution time frames, and establishing consequences for unmet commitments, possibly allowing contract termination or a service credit. Default SLAs aim to provide acceptable service while limiting MSSP liabilities, but they may have vague aspects, such as unclear timelines for alert delivery. Regular metric reviews, independent monitoring, and adjusting SLAs as your business evolves are key considerations.

Case study 2: Document requirements

Let's revisit our InfoSec team to see how they outlined their requirements. They had chosen to outsource two non-core tasks, namely creating user accounts and resetting passwords, considering them a preliminary test before committing to larger outsourcing endeavors. These tasks were significant enough to capture attention but not so critical that failure would be catastrophic for the team or the company. To determine the required responsiveness, the team consulted operational business leaders, resulting in specific outcomes: password resets within 60 minutes and user account creation within four hours of the initial request. Despite initial unease about relinquishing control, the team, driven by the prospect of focusing more on core tasks, proceeded with their outsourcing initiative with confidence in their risk management capabilities.

What is an MSSP?

Managed Security Service Provider (MSSP) originated from the Internet Service Providers of the 1990s, MSSPs initially offered hardware-based firewalls to customers, remotely managing them for an additional fee. Over time, MSSPs expanded their services to include various security offerings like intrusion detection systems, incident response, and vulnerability assessments. Forester, a leading industry research firm, identified significant MSSPs in the global market in 2018. Despite the capabilities of MSSPs, the customer retains ultimate responsibility for its security. The relationship between the MSSP and the customer isn't a simple turnkey arrangement; customers need to actively manage, monitor, and hold the MSSP accountable for contracted services.

Recognize and manage conflicting goals—profit vs. outcomes

When collaborating with an MSSP, your primary focus is achieving excellent outcomes for your non-core tasks. However, it's crucial to recognize that the MSSP's primary goal is maintaining steady, profitable growth, which may conflict with your pursuit of thorough and high-quality services. The tension arises when the vendor aims to cut corners to boost profits while hoping you won't notice. An example is intrusion detection system monitoring, where the MSSP may be incentivized to minimize the number of events it investigates to reduce costs. This poses a risk of false negatives; genuine alarms being dismissed as false. To mitigate this risk, delve into understanding how the MSSP performs the delegated tasks and consider implementing a verification mechanism for the reports received.

How do I evaluate an MSSP?

When evaluating an MSSP, prioritize the following criteria:

1. Features and functions of the service.

2. Business structure and practices.

3. Security measures at their site.

Key aspects to consider include the effectiveness of their solution, reporting capabilities, default availability and scalability, cost, independent evaluations (e.g., SOC2), transition and implementation plans, and exit strategy.

Assess their business by examining the location's stability, working hours alignment, cultural fit, financial health, and customer satisfaction. A site visit may be beneficial to verify claims and observe adherence to physical security protocols, providing insights into operationalizing your policies.

Case study 3: Select a vendor

Let's revisit our InfoSec team to explore their MSSP selection process, step three in their plan. Focusing on user account creation and password reset as a proof of concept, they set specific response times: 60 minutes for password resets and four hours for user account creation. To address conflicting goals, they discovered the MSSP already performed these tasks for other clients, verifying default procedures. A team member visited the MSSP's office, conducting a screenshare walkthrough with the home team. Although the MSSP's tools excelled in service ticket and remote management, the InfoSec team noticed a lack of information security training or certifications in the MSSP staff. Despite initial unease, the MSSP displayed operational discipline, agreed to procedural changes at no extra cost, and the SLA included reimbursement for incidents caused by the MSSP. Ultimately, the InfoSec team felt confident in proceeding with the outsourcing process.

How do I contract with a vendor?

Ensuring an accurate contract with your MSSP is vital. I am not providing legal advice, but based on experience, negotiating a contract without a qualified attorney or contracts manager is unwise, as contracts may not function as expected. Adopting a "set it and forget it" approach to outsourcing is problematic; your needs and the outsourcing landscape regularly change. For instance, recent pricing model shifts in MSSPs, embracing cloud computing and machine learning, have led to more cost-effective services. Therefore, contracts must be flexible to capitalize on favorable trends. Consider your contracting strategy as a lifecycle with a beginning, middle, and end, potentially followed by a new beginning. This involves entering into a deal, working under specific terms, revising or terminating the contract, and starting anew. Key contract features include termination for convenience, regular performance reviews, audit rights, and financial reimbursement, also known as indemnification, in case of a data breach. Seek assistance from an experienced lawyer or contracts manager for effective contract management.

Tips for contracting with a vendor

To ensure the right contract with your MSSP, follow these tips:

1. Utilize a responsibility assignment matrix (e.g., RACI) to clarify roles and responsibilities, reducing the risk of deviation from procedures over time.

2. Decide whether to use your contract or evaluate and modify the MSSP's contract, considering templates used by experienced outsourcing organizations.

3. Implement supply chain risk management, incorporating your MSSP into your third-party risk management program and assessing them routinely.

4. Require MSSP protection of sensitive data, including termination options for non-compliance, and establish a financial firewall by making them liable for breach costs.

5. Retain a sense of ownership over cybersecurity risk rather than attempting to transfer all responsibilities to the MSSP.

Case study 4: Contract with the vendor

Returning to our InfoSec team's progress, in the fourth step of contracting with the MSSP, they selected their preferred MSSP after thorough evaluations. Upon scrutinizing the MSSP's standard contract with their in-house contracts manager, the team found it unfavorable and opted to create their own template. Despite initial reluctance from the MSSP about using an alternate contract, they agreed due to potential future collaborations. Negotiations ensued, and once the terms were settled, the contract underwent a final review by an external attorney and was duly signed by both parties. The InfoSec team was pleased to have advanced this far in the outsourcing process.

Plan and perform transition to the vendor

A successful transition to your MSSP relies on two key factors: the people involved and the tasks they undertake. Obtain and scrutinize your MSSP's standard transition plan, ensuring it aligns with your specific needs. Assign the most experienced individuals from both sides to handle the transition, recognizing that the people dimension is a crucial risk factor. Support your team through the change by maintaining a strong focus on their roles within the new responsibility matrix. Effective communication, using various channels, is vital to keep everyone informed and aligned. Schedule MSSP performance review meetings in advance, holding them more frequently during the initial weeks post-transition to promptly address any issues. Additionally, conduct testing on the service to validate its performance, such as submitting unconventional requests or performing penetration tests. This proactive approach ensures a smooth operational shift and helps guarantee the desired outcomes.

Tips for transitioning to the vendor

Have a clear plan for managing your relationship with the MSSP to mitigate the risk of destructive conflicts that can jeopardize collaboration. Establish an effective escalation procedure to address tough conflicts and avoid damaging relationships. The primary challenge in outsourcing lies in interpersonal relationships within your team and with the outsourced team. Recognize that outsourcing can impact your organization's culture, potentially for the better or worse. Changes in how work is done and who it involves can create uncertainty and fear. As a leader, guide your team through each stage, provide transparency about the changes, and treat individuals respectfully, allowing them the time and support needed to process the transition.

Case study 5: Implement the agreement

Our infosec team successfully transitioned the work to their MSSP in step five of the process. On the cutover date, the MSSP took over the tasks, and to ensure compliance, the infosec team gained access to a monitoring console and installed an event-logging database for direct insights. Daily performance reviews in the first week transitioned to weekly reviews for the next two months. To facilitate the transition, they collaborated with marketing to create a comprehensive internal communications plan. This included strategic communication objectives linking outsourcing to core business goals, clear explanations of what was outsourced, benefits for affected individuals, and success indicators. The information was disseminated through email, internal newsletters, intranet videos, and Q&A sessions in department meetings. They also partnered with HR to train supervisors and managers on emotional transitions, provide generous layoff packages, and encourage open communication for addressing questions and concerns.

Manage by Service Level Agreements (SLA)

After the transition, resist the temptation to disengage from the MSSP and solely focus on core tasks. Your organization bears the consequences of MSSP failure, so monitoring their performance through the SLA is crucial. A well-planned contract includes clear SLA terms, effective metrics, and regular reporting, along with robust penalty provisions for violations. Utilize these provisions to deter performance lapses and, with effective monitoring tools, address issues proactively. Keep a vigilant eye on performance metrics, encourage feedback from stakeholders, celebrate successes, and explore avenues for improvement. If SLA violations occur, prompt action is essential.

Manage by contractual terms

The SLA identifies issues, while contractual terms offer remedies or an exit strategy. A well-prepared contract includes termination for convenience, regular performance reviews, audit rights, indemnification for data breaches, and financial penalties for non-performance. Penalty size may vary; smaller penalties for lower-cost services, like 10%, and larger ones for significant expenses. Amazon Web Services illustrates escalating service credits for downtime, ranging from small to 100%. While you can impose penalties, view the MSSP as a partner, encourage improvement, and be prepared to dissolve the agreement if necessary.

Case study 6: Manage the vendor

Our Infosec team effectively managed their MSSP in step six. They tracked vendor response times through reports and conducted independent reviews using timestamps in the ticketing system and system logs. Over time, they deciphered crucial data and considered feedback from direct interactions. Initially challenging, they learned to delegate work through the MSSP, requiring self-restraint and adaptability. Ongoing guidance from the corporate contracts manager proved valuable. The major issue arose when the MSSP violated security practices by storing passwords in their ticketing system. Strong SLA penalties corrected this behavior, leading to the implementation of a secure self-password reset system.

How to renew the agreement

During contract renewal, you hold a favorable position with your MSSP, with the ability to continue, cease, or renegotiate terms. It's essential to approach this process carefully. Approximately 60 days before the contract expires, decide whether to extend or renew, considering potential changes in services or service levels. Note that renewal opens all terms for renegotiation, while an extension maintains existing terms with a prolonged expiration date. If opting not to renew, prepare for a challenging conversation with your MSSP, especially if they've made efforts to meet your requirements. Always seek legal advice during contract negotiations.

When to not renew the agreement

Consider not renewing your MSSP agreement if you observe signs of poor performance, strained relationships, resistance to necessary changes, or unfavorable renewal terms. Ending the contract requires understanding the termination process, as it may involve challenges like evergreen clauses, which automatically extend the contract. Be aware of these clauses and navigate them accordingly to ensure a smooth termination.

Case study 7: Renew the agreement

The Infosec team had a challenging start with their MSSP but experienced overall satisfaction in the first year of outsourcing. No layoffs occurred, and despite initial anxiety, the team improved efficiency in handling core tasks. They viewed the first year as a learning experience, leading to a renewed agreement with significant changes to the SLA section. Encouraged by the positive outcomes, they expanded their outsourcing collaboration to three MSSPs, effectively outsourcing most of their tactical and strategic tasks. The team considered outsourcing a successful decision and hoped for continued success in the future.

Chapter 6 Building Your Cybersecurity Talent Pipeline
The cybersecurity skills gap: Fact or fiction?

The cybersecurity skills gap persists, posing a major challenge for the industry. Despite efforts to address it, studies indicate the gap will likely grow, creating difficulties for security leaders in recruiting and retaining talent. According to ISC-squared's 2021 workforce study, 60% of participants see the skills shortage as the primary barrier to meeting organizational security needs. While there is a surge in individuals entering the cybersecurity field to bridge the gap, many struggle to secure employment due to various factors, such as lack of experience, non-technical backgrounds, and inadequate education or certification.

This creates a paradox—on one side, a high demand for qualified talent in a competitive market, and on the other side, entry-level talent finding it challenging to secure roles. The disconnect prompts questions about whether job seekers should enhance their qualifications, if hiring managers should reconsider requirements, or if security leaders should reshape cybersecurity programs to accommodate professionals at all levels. The suggested solution involves restructuring security teams to create opportunities for entry-level talent, defining qualifications based on role functions, and fostering collaboration among certification bodies, academic institutions, and industry needs. This approach benefits both job seekers and security teams, influencing decisions of certification bodies and academic institutions, ultimately benefiting the entire cybersecurity ecosystem. While implementing such changes may seem challenging, we'll explore common challenges faced by security leaders and provide insights on solving them, emphasizing the importance of aligning team priorities with organizational goals to achieve desired outcomes.

Hiring doesn't have to be hard

Experience—a valuable asset, especially in the cybersecurity field where the stakes are high for protecting corporate assets. The need for talent is critical, but the cybersecurity industry faces the challenge of top talent having the luxury to choose from numerous companies seeking security personnel. This reality requires leaders and hiring managers to be creative, broaden their search, and enhance their recruitment strategies.

Using a shopping analogy, the importance of choosing the path of least resistance in talent acquisition is emphasized. Instead of standing in the longest line, representing a saturated market, hiring managers should explore less saturated markets and consider entry-level talent. While concerns about the risk of hiring candidates with little experience are valid, the solution lies in mitigating this risk by creating opportunities for grooming newcomers with the right skill set.

The approach involves structuring teams to enable the development of entry-level talent. By defining roles with granularity and considering the difference between enabling a junior resource with the right skills over time versus hiring a more expensive mid-level resource, leaders can make informed decisions that benefit both talent development and organizational success.

Retention is critical

Retaining cybersecurity talent is becoming almost as challenging as hiring in the industry. While specific retention strategies will be discussed later, it's crucial to understand the importance of retention. Referring back to the team's top priority and roles helps security leaders stay focused on the team's mission. The overall mission, like reducing cyber risk or maintaining compliance, involves continuous development, monitoring, measurement, and improvement over time.

Retention becomes significant because long-term employees gain a deep understanding of business requirements, internal processes, and technology solutions. Their historical context and experience provide valuable insights for decision-making in cybersecurity. Long-term employees are invaluable to a security team, and losing them can hinder program maturity and improvement. Retaining mid to senior-level talent is easier and more beneficial than dealing with the challenges of hiring and onboarding new resources, especially at a critical level.

Defining roles and responsibilities

A pipeline staffing approach involves expanding the talent pool with entry-level opportunities and retaining mid to senior-level talent. To start, leaders and hiring managers need to be more granular in defining responsibilities for each role on the team. A brief break from cybersecurity pressure illustrates Amanda's experience at Cake Design. Initially hiring experienced cake designers, Amanda faced challenges when they left for more exciting work. Shifting to hiring junior talent, she listed basic tasks for a junior baker, allowing the head baker to groom them over time. This approach proved successful, providing operational efficiencies and readiness for increased responsibility. Similarly, granular role definitions in security teams lower barriers for newcomers and establish an internal pipeline.

Putting in the work

Chris, the newly appointed Chief Information Security Officer at Bank International, has tasked us with defining a role for the internal security operations center (SOC). Chris liked our pipeline mentality and sent a list of responsibilities for a SOC analyst role. To tackle this, we'll use the LEADERS framework in seven steps. First, list the top 5-10 responsibilities (already done). Second, establish evaluation criteria such as criticality, risk, and training requirements. Third, assess responsibilities against criteria using a basic ranking system (e.g., high, medium, low). Fourth, identify any broad items in the list and expand them into sub-items. Fifth, reassess and modify rankings. Sixth, specify which responsibilities align with each skill level, considering the assessment outcomes. Lastly, make decisions on skill levels for each responsibility. This framework is versatile and can be applied to mid and senior-level roles. We've successfully created room for entry-level talent. Well done! Looking forward to Chris's feedback.

Job descriptions: The good, the bad, and the ugly

It's crucial for organizations to refine these descriptions to better prepare and attract talent. Our friend Chris at Global Bank International wants us to review entry-level job descriptions. Exhibit one exemplifies an unclear fit for entry-level talent, overwhelming with diverse responsibilities. Prioritizing essential skills and marking others as nice-to-haves can enhance clarity. Exhibit two highlights the mistake of requiring advanced certifications (CISA, CISSP) with extensive experience for an entry-level position. Using certifications like Security+ or Network+ aligns better with the technical nature of the role.

Maintaining your pipeline

Building a talent pipeline is an ongoing and challenging process, especially in today's competitive job market. However, the journey doesn't end with defining entry-level opportunities and creating appealing job postings. It extends to maintaining the pipeline by constantly assessing and nurturing the talent within it. Similar to attracting customers to a consulting business, attracting and retaining top candidates requires presenting a compelling offer that sets your company apart. Talent pipeline maintenance is essential for success, but it can become more efficient over time with effective strategies.

Career progression as a program strategy

When seeking local vendors or service providers in a new neighborhood, your decision is influenced by various factors such as prices, business hours, and staff likability. Similarly, vendors need to understand the key influencers to attract their target market. Buyers have the upper hand, choosing businesses aligning with their preferences. This dynamic applies to entry-level talent in the cybersecurity field. Candidates, like new neighbors, consider motivators like salary, work arrangements, and team dynamics. As leaders, understanding these influencers helps attract and retain talent. Candidates prioritize factors like training, continuous learning, and growth opportunities, indicating a desire for career progression. Highlighting these aspects in job descriptions or interviews can set your team apart and create a win-win scenario for both the candidate and the organization.

Defining career progression requirements

Before delving into growth plans, it's essential to establish career progression requirements. These requirements outline the skills needed to advance within a specific role. For simplicity, let's focus on progression within a security consultant role, categorizing skills into security and interpersonal categories. At each level (entry, mid, and senior), specific skills and key performance indicators are defined. Level one requires foundational security knowledge and the ability to establish working relationships. At level two, the consultant must demonstrate intermediate security knowledge, achieve trusted advisor status, and obtain certifications. The senior level demands expert security skills, advanced certifications, and proactive engagement in interpersonal skills. These requirements serve as tangible criteria for career advancement, providing clarity for employees. However, to address the "how" aspect, a growth plan is needed to guide individuals in meeting these requirements.

Creating growth plans and investing in your team

Top-performing, high-potential team members are driven to enhance their performance and advance their careers, akin to elevating their game. While clearly defined career progression requirements are crucial for motivation, merely outlining them can make team members feel unsupported or see the next career step as unattainable. These plans detail identified gaps, strategies to address them, milestones, key performance indicators, and available resources. For example, if an entry-level resource meets mid-level requirements but lacks a certification, a growth plan could set a target date, provide training, and schedule progress discussions. Similarly, if the employee wishes to switch teams, the plan might involve shadowing opportunities for skill development. This approach benefits both employee motivation and team skill enhancement.

Boosting your corporate brand

When discussing career growth, a common misconception is that personal brand is only about public image. Many focus on external branding, neglecting their internal brand built through workplace interactions. For security leaders and teams, while the company has an external brand, internally, employees' perceptions matter. Their views on the company's culture, leadership, and mission influence their engagement. In hiring and recruiting, you and your team are a sub-brand of the corporate brand. Aligning with it, you need unique differentiators to attract talent. Focusing on both personal leadership brand and team brand has proven successful in talent attraction and retention. Being a leader worth following and fostering an inclusive, growth-oriented team culture helps build a positive reputation. Externally, visibility is valuable—share insights, successes, and team updates to humanize technical roles. Internally, craft a mission statement, create excitement, and make employees feel part of something great to boost morale and foster employee-driven talent acquisition.

Return on investment

If you're committed to creating opportunities for industry newcomers, convincing other organizational leaders is crucial. Program effectiveness, often tied to perceived security, should consider stability and maturity linked to day-to-day security operations teams. Business justification should include the security program's ROI, going beyond financial metrics to assess program volatility. High volatility, with turnover and open roles, poses risks, while low volatility, with a well-staffed, skilled team, enhances stability. Creating an external pool of entry-level talent can boost stability, maturity, and ROI, correlating the program's effectiveness with the security team's performance.

Chapter 7 Building a Cybersecurity Awareness Program

Getting to know the teams

Initiate your security awareness program by fostering relationships with various teams to grasp their security needs. Start by connecting with key figures like the CISO, CIO, or your direct manager, who set performance expectations and provide essential support. Understand and collaborate with the security team to gain insights into the current threat landscape and organizational security roadmap. Engage with the IT team to access valuable statistics related to employee risks, such as help desk tickets on malicious emails, suspicious activity, and device issues. Partner with Human Resources for organizational insights like headcount, employee distribution, titles, etc., crucial for training and awareness initiatives.

Collaborate with Legal to align policies with company regulations, and secure approval for documents and communications. Work closely with Corporate Communications or Marketing for internal communications and content reviews, benefiting from their graphic design and messaging expertise. Explore connections with teams like Risk, Compliance, Audit, Physical Security, Facilities, and Learning Management, tailoring your program to meet the unique needs of each team. Building relationships with various groups from the start ensures a comprehensive and effective security awareness program, emphasizing its collaborative nature.

Understanding company policies

Security policy documentation safeguards a company, its employees, and assets. While the responsibility of developing and maintaining policies may not directly fall under the security awareness role, close alignment with these documents and their custodians is crucial. A comprehensive understanding of administrative and technical controls outlined in these policies is essential. Familiarize yourself with all security policies to effectively communicate and train employees on them. Read policy documents from an end user's perspective to ensure clear communication to individuals with minimal security or technical knowledge. Even if your organization already has security training, verify that it aligns with your company's policies. Ensure employees review and accept relevant policies annually, attaching it to existing training or using another method for compliance tracking.

Consider creating in-house training sessions specifically addressing company policy documents as your program matures. For organizations with numerous policies, a high-level employee security handbook can serve as a digestible summary guide without replacing detailed policies. Regularly update training to reflect new policy changes, and consistently communicate any alterations affecting employees' daily work. It is imperative for every employee to comprehend and adhere to company security policies to minimize potential security threats and vulnerabilities. Stay informed about policy documents to effectively convey their content to all employees in an easily understandable manner.

Survey employees to understand threats

To create an effective program, understanding the daily experiences, existing knowledge, and learning interests of the employees you're training is crucial. Use surveys to gauge this information, keeping them short with 10 to 20 questions. Ensure broad participation, including leadership, and consider demographic-specific questions. Ask about awareness of the security team, knowledge of social engineering, and preferences for communication. Anonymity may encourage more honest feedback. If participation is low, consider incentives like gift cards. Analyze survey results to guide security awareness initiatives, addressing gaps in employee knowledge. Share results with employees to demonstrate the impact of their input. Conduct annual surveys to track changes and cultural shifts. Additionally, collaborate with the incident response (IR) team to understand the current threat landscape. Regular meetings, access to dashboards, and participation in IR activities will keep you informed. Security awareness is not only essential for risk awareness but also plays a vital role in incident response by keeping the organization updated on emerging threats affecting employees at work and at home.

Developing a program plan

Once you've assessed the current state of your program and familiarized yourself with policies and risks, the next step is planning. Start with a 30-day focus on team interactions, relationships, and understanding the program and business. Document your plan, aligning expectations with leadership. Move to a 90-day plan with goals like team branding, employee surveys, campaign ideas, and phishing test concepts. Your one-year plan includes quarterly campaigns, annual training, and more. For the three-year vision, consider refining, updating, and expanding security offerings, such as re-surveying employees, demonstrating metric changes, tailoring phishing training, and establishing a security liaison program. Organize plans using charts or task sheets, and keep the document fluid, adapting it to evolving needs and risks.

Understanding your budget

When creating a budget for your security awareness program, start by understanding the overall security budget or the budget of the team you report to. Create short-term and long-term budgets outlining realistic costs for themes like technology/tools, people/resources, and tangible support items. Consider costs for software, learning management systems, training content, phishing simulation tools, additional hardware, memberships, and external speakers. People/resources costs may include additional staff, interns, or fees for external support. Tangible support items involve prizes, gift cards, posters, and promotional items. Justify your budget request with statistics, metrics, and potential cost avoidance in case of a security breach. If your initial request is limited, be creative with low-budget approaches, but emphasize the return on investment and cost avoidance to secure necessary buy-in and budget approval.

Developing a brand

Creating a brand for your security team fosters easy identification of communications and training, enhancing trust and shaping your team's perception. While not mandatory, a brand distinguishes your group and its communications. Start by establishing a team name aligned with your mission, then create a dedicated team email address for consistent communication. Designing a logo adds a visually memorable element to your brand, aiding recognition and content ownership. Introduce a catchy catchphrase or slogan to further differentiate your team. When everything is approved, unveil the new brand with an event, distributing branded swag and communicating through your new email address. This branding strategy ensures consistent and easily recognizable messaging, establishing your security team as a trusted asset in your organization.

Creating traditional training

When developing security training for employees, consider various methods such as video, computer-based, live sessions, webinars, games, and quizzes. Aim to incorporate multiple forms of training as budget and time allow. Annual training should cover the main risks and threats, with three approaches to consider: third-party, in-house, or a hybrid of both. Initiate security education during onboarding, providing tools for good security habits. Conduct required annual security awareness training for all personnel accessing company systems. Implement ongoing training aligned with incident response events, phishing campaigns, and high-risk occurrences. Create a training program calendar for planning and execution, aligning with monthly themes and events. Utilize methods like company intranet, email, and newsletters to promote and track training. Tailor training to specific groups, regions, and technical levels for a more mature and culturally impactful program.

Finding security champions and liaisons

Leverage established relationships with groups to create an internal network of security liaisons, advocates, and champions. Begin by conducting an in-house meeting with your security team and leaders to identify key groups and individuals. Market the security awareness extension group as an exciting opportunity for employees to play a vital role in securing the company. Choose enthusiastic individuals with a baseline knowledge of security, ensuring representation across global locations if applicable. Survey advocates to understand their specific security needs and tailor communication and training accordingly. Establish ongoing, two-way communication channels with advocates through meetings, instant messaging, emails, blogs, or an internal site. Promote the security advocate team within the company, featuring names and photos on internal web pages, sending email announcements, and providing branded giveaways. Make the advocate role exciting to encourage engagement and expand the program as your security awareness efforts grow.

Creating nontraditional training

Aside from conventional training methods, explore alternative ways to engage and educate your employees on security. Implement ongoing training through quarterly campaigns and consider additional methods. Choose a relevant topic by leveraging survey feedback and insights from your Incident Response (IR) team. Research other organizations' training topics and include themes that impact employees personally. Craft catchy verbiage, incorporating lessons for an educational experience. Collaborate with designers to create visually appealing posters aligned with company branding. Print and distribute posters in high-traffic areas, ensuring visibility. Convert the poster concept into a screensaver with the help of technical experts. Create newsletters featuring external content, team-written articles, and contributions from the Chief Information Security Officer (CISO). Establish dedicated intranet pages with links to resources and conduct tabletop exercises or informational tables in common areas. Utilize various methods such as quizzes, games, and giveaways to engage employees. Deploy all campaign elements simultaneously for a coordinated and impactful launch. Evaluate the campaign's effectiveness and prepare for the next quarter with a new theme.

Finding creative ways to brand

Ensure a strategic approach to communicating high-risk events, tailoring delivery methods for effectiveness. Collaborate with the internal communications team to develop a communications plan, leveraging their expertise. Limit direct email for major issues, keeping messages concise and linking to additional content if necessary. Utilize the company internet by requesting a security awareness subpage for document library purposes. Alternatively, create an internal blog with the security team for announcements and updates. Establish a separate instant messaging channel for security interactions with employees, fostering open communication. Leverage social media, private or public, for communication, especially during Security Awareness Month. Seek employee input through surveys on preferred communication methods, considering group or region-specific preferences. Enhance the visibility of the security team by diversifying communication channels based on employee feedback.

Conducting social engineering tests

Phishing simulations provide hands-on training to assess employee knowledge, but they are just one element of a comprehensive security program. To initiate a social engineering test, draw inspiration from real threats, such as reported emails or phishing attempts. Plan the test deployment, considering third-party resources or internal creation, and inform relevant teams and executives. Choose an optimal go-live date, gather metrics based on the test type, and provide immediate education to participants. Avoid shaming and turn any mistakes into learning opportunities. Communicate results with executives using dashboards and visuals. Develop a simulation calendar for regular testing, allowing for more tailored simulations as the program matures. Simulations offer practical training and insights, helping refine overall security awareness efforts.

Developing an annual training event

Organizing an annual security awareness event can engage employees with alternative training formats. Begin by planning the event's format, whether a day, week, or multiple smaller events. Consider logistical details, securing a location, and budgeting for giveaways, speakers, and technology. Develop a schedule with internal and external speakers, covering both work and personal security topics. Market the event a month in advance, creating enticing promotional material and offering prizes. For a global audience, ensure diverse representation and provide options for remote attendance through live streaming or webinars. If a large-scale event is challenging, explore smaller alternatives like coffee sessions or outdoor activities. Foster creativity with escape rooms, card games, and simulations to make learning enjoyable. Collect feedback and metrics to refine future events and reinforce the importance of security awareness for all employees.

Making the security team accessible

Foster continuous engagement between the security team and employees through various channels. Utilize existing events like team meetings, town halls, and employee engagement activities to inject security-related content. Tailor presentations for different departments by gathering feedback through questionnaires. Schedule talks or set up a table at all-company meetings to share educational materials and giveaways. Integrate security into employee engagement events and team-building activities by creating games or providing prizes. Keep reaching out to diverse groups, regions, and leadership to identify opportunities for tailored training and communications. Leverage a security email box for employees to report concerns and encourage individualized responses. Utilize blogs, instant messenger, newsletters, and other communication methods to enhance visibility for the security team. Celebrate team achievements and certifications to showcase ongoing efforts in enhancing knowledge. Establish open communication to build trust, allowing employees to feel comfortable reporting incidents and viewing security as a positive resource.

Measuring cultural change

When evaluating the effectiveness of security awareness programs, consider metrics beyond mere training completion. Measure the success by tracking voluntary enrollments in additional security training, demonstrating a genuine interest in security. Utilize an LMS to monitor enrollment and completion rates for supplementary offerings. Gauge the impact of communications by tracking click rates on links and traffic to internal pages. Monitor event attendance, both required and voluntary, showcasing growth as the program evolves. Leverage communication channels like blogs or instant messaging to track participation, identifying trends in employee interests. Utilize the security mailbox not only for reporting malicious emails but also for tracking questions and demonstrating employees' ability to identify threats. While phishing simulation click rates are essential, prioritize tracking the report rate in various social engineering tests. A true cultural shift is evident when employees identify threats and know whom to report them to. Measure a shift in security culture by tracking requests from employees seeking additional resources, information, or training. Be creative in finding diverse ways to measure program effectiveness, tailoring metrics to your organization's context and program maturity. Consistently track data to showcase genuine security cultural change.

What can you do with the metrics

Leverage the plethora of metrics you've gathered to benefit your security awareness program. Share these metrics with your immediate security team, presenting them through eye-catching infographics and dashboards. Discuss solutions to improve identified gaps and emphasize the role the security team can play. Extend the sharing to employees, fostering dialogue and highlighting their impact on the program's success. Communicate both negative and positive metrics, clarifying goals and encouraging continuous improvement. Share these metrics with C-level leadership to underscore the importance of employee education in cybersecurity. Consider disseminating the information to the board, led by high-level management. Utilize the metrics to demonstrate cost avoidance rather than ROI, emphasizing the potential losses from a data breach. Use the metrics to request a larger budget, additional resources (including personnel, technology, and third-party vendors), and support for expanding or enhancing your program. Empower your program with data-driven insights, gaining buy-in at all organizational levels and showcasing the effectiveness of security training.

Next steps

Elevate your security awareness program by understanding diverse learning styles and the psychology of your learners. Adapt and customize your program continuously, tailoring communications, training, and phishing tests to specific audiences for maximum impact. Align internal content with company policies, covering a wide range of evolving cybersecurity topics. Stay creative and research-driven to proactively address emerging threats. Strive for continuous program maturity and effectiveness, demonstrating growth year over year. Acknowledge that while 100% prevention isn't possible, empowering employees through training enhances overall security. Embrace the people-centric nature of security awareness, inspiring individuals to contribute to a more secure workplace and world. Keep learning and maintain the passion to foster a safer environment.

Chapter 8 Crisis Communication Planning After a Cybersecurity Attack

Why cyberattacks impact every organization

Have you ever thought, "That won't happen to me"? Many businesses share this sentiment, especially when it comes to cyber threats like ransomware. Some believe they are too small to be targeted. However, cyber attackers don't discriminate based on company size; internet connectivity is all they need. In fact, an attack may have already occurred, with cyber criminals lurking in systems for weeks or months before making their move. Ransomware is a growing threat, hitting businesses every 11 seconds, costing $20 billion in 2021, and expected to reach $10.5 trillion in damages globally by 2025. Small and mid-size businesses are particularly vulnerable, facing potential closure within six months post-attack. Employees play a significant role in these incidents, often unintentionally aiding cyber criminals. Communication during a crisis is crucial, as highlighted by examples of a large oil pipeline company and a small physicians group facing negative publicity due to inadequate responses. A well-prepared crisis communication plan can make a vital difference, preserving your organization's reputation and viability.

Determining who is on your team when a cyberattack occurs

In planning for communication during a cyberattack, engage every department to ensure effective coordination. Initiate collaboration with the legal team, maintaining attorney-client privilege, and involving them in communication activities. Coordinate with IT and information security teams to understand response elements, especially if outsourced. Establish rapport with the HR team for access to employees. Involve the board of directors and senior management at a high level. Regularly coordinate with all departments as depicted in the chart. Engage them before an attack to understand their setup for security breaches. Ask legal about forensic investigation initiation, law enforcement relationships, etc. Query IT about identifying infiltration origin, forensics, and system recovery. Inquire HR about policies, employee investigations, and communication tools. Your crisis communications team should address breach notifications, priority audiences, and message content. Review and share practices and processes with departments to enhance readiness. Keep communication lines open and established for effective response.

What to say and to whom at onset

Upon receiving a ransomware note, prompt communication with various audiences is crucial. Prioritize audiences: employees, customers, business partners, government entities, investors/donors, and press/public. Employees should be informed first, being your valuable marketing asset. Decide whether to proactively communicate or wait for inquiries, considering legal, regulatory, and potential backlash factors. Be prepared to shift to an active mode if needed. Balance transparency without jeopardizing negotiations or legal concerns. Communicate specific details without sounding ambiguous or evasive. Be mindful of tone and body language, offering assurance and commitment. Incorporate empathy and action in each message, reinforcing key messages. Provide regular updates on security measures and investigations, emphasizing the priority of information security.

Prepare your team to address a crisis

In preparing your crisis communication team for a cybersecurity crisis, maintain regular meetings with senior leadership and the crisis communication team to discuss ongoing developments. Continuously update your plan based on the latest information. Identify effective spokespeople during the cyber-attack and provide regular feedback to enhance their effectiveness. Evaluate spokespeople based on their ability to recall messaging, display empathy, convey professionalism through body language, and express confidence. Coordinate messaging across social media and press releases, updating social media channels frequently. Prepare for inbound queries from various channels and be ready for challenging questions, avoiding a "no comment" response. Assess your organization's response time to inquiries and strive to stay on topic. Adaptability is crucial, requiring regular updates to your crisis communication plan as the situation evolves. Stay proactive in communication and be prepared for inevitable changes during a cyber-attack.

Coordinate responses with all departments and ask the following questions to ensure a comprehensive approach:

Legal:

1. Who initiates the forensics investigation, and how does it unfold?

2. How are relationships with law enforcement agencies established and maintained?

3. What is the company's stance on negotiating with threat actors?

4. Who initiates negotiations if decided upon?

5. Who manages required breach notifications to third parties?

InfoSec and IT Teams:

1. How do you identify the origin of the infiltration ("patient zero")?

2. What's the process for conducting the forensics investigation?

3. How are backup systems activated or the current system decrypted?

4. How are security holes patched?

5. How do you coordinate efforts with legal and the rest of the team?

Human Resources:

1. What policies cover information security and IT investigations involving employees?

2. Who conducts these investigations?

3. What communication tools does HR use regularly?

4. Who in HR is responsible for disseminating information?

Crisis Communications Team:

1. What's required for customer breach notifications and by whom?

2. Which audience groups (employees, customers, partners, investors, etc.) take priority in communications?

3. What messages will be conveyed?

4. Under what circumstances will information be proactively disseminated?

5. When will you wait to respond to queries before releasing information?

6. Who serves as a spokesperson, and to which audiences?

7. How will inquiries be handled?

Practice to improve crisis communications

To enhance communication effectiveness during crises like ransomware incidents, practicing and developing muscle memory with your team is crucial. Failure to practice responses, especially to challenging questions, may lead to reactive behaviors, either adopting a confrontational stance ("fight mode") or remaining silent ("flight mode"). The "fight mode" can escalate tension and hinder a return to normal operations, as exemplified by SolarWinds blaming an intern for a cyber breach. Conversely, "flight mode" — staying silent or providing vague answers — may portray your organization as incompetent or indifferent. For instance, a US health company's delayed and vague response to a cyber-attack resulted in prolonged animosity and trust issues. Effectively conveying your message in a thoughtful and well-understood manner is vital for connecting with audiences and garnering their support.

What to tell people after the attack

After identifying and resolving the source of the cyber breach, particularly in cases of ransomware, ongoing communication with target audiences is essential. Update customers regularly on the investigation progress and findings. Failing to make this effort can lead to continued negative publicity, as seen with SolarWinds, a tech company that faced repercussions a year later for blaming an employee and subsequent missteps. Maintain monthly communications for at least three months after the incident, providing insights into the breach's extent, compromised information, and prevention measures. Ensure open lines of communication to instill confidence, and collaborate with the legal team to mitigate liability risks. Utilize this time for positive campaigns showcasing enhanced security measures, as demonstrated by companies that successfully communicated their efforts. Communication must persist even after the attack is resolved to meet the expectations of clients, employees, investors, supporters, and partners, safeguarding your reputation.

Continue to evaluate after a training

After the crisis concludes, assess your communication performance for resilience and improvement opportunities. Promptly query your communications team about preparedness, effective tactics, potential additions to future incident responses, and identify proficient and underperforming spokespeople. Evaluate how well messaging was received, the speed of inquiry routing, and response times. Conduct post-crisis evaluations while the events are fresh in your memory and gather candid feedback from various departments through discussions, meetings, and surveys. Incorporate this feedback into the communication plan, updating messaging, tactics, timelines, and addressing potential gotcha questions. Share the revised plan to familiarize stakeholders with communication changes during a cyber-attack. Although revisiting a crisis may seem daunting, periodic evaluations, especially after cyber events, enhance preparedness and effectiveness for future incidents.

Design crisis scenario-based training for higher retention

Effective training is crucial due to the high likelihood of a cyber-attack on your organization. Include anyone involved in internal or external communication in the training. Utilize scenario-based and situational training with mock interviews, presenting realistic cases for problem-solving in a safe environment. Structure the training to cover what to say, with whom, when, by whom, coordination efforts, keeping PR updated, and the duration of crisis PR mode. Practical training ensures better retention of information. Examples of scenarios include a breach affecting employee data and a ransomware incident with customer complaints and media speculation. Learn from others' experiences and incorporate lessons into your training. Conduct one to two-hour sessions with mock interviews and audience conversations, concluding with feedback and celebration. This not only enhances communication skills during cyber-attacks but also fosters a positive work environment.

You can do this

Crisis communication events bring disruptions to operations, HR, customer relations, and reputation management. The goal in facing unexpected cyber threats is resiliency. To build a resilient plan, prioritize being proactive, delivering clear, empathetic, action-oriented messaging to all audiences, not just news organizations. This approach minimizes damage and speeds up the return to normal operations. Planning and practicing, though often in short supply, are crucial. Poorly managed crisis communication strategies have, unfortunately, led to the downfall of numerous businesses.

www.ingramcontent.com/pod-product-compliance
Lightning Source LLC
LaVergne TN
LVHW051616050326
832903LV00033B/4526